I'm sure this was a hard book for Abdu [

important and insightful book to read. / [

with questions about the interaction of [

SAM ALLBERRY, pastor

Over the last few years, I've had the privilege of getting to know Abdu and his heart for people. Without a doubt he's one of the best at diving deep to answer tough questions in a clear way. His background, compassionate approach, and passion for Jesus gives him the unique ability to impact people all over the world.

TIM TEBOW, former NFL quarterback and author of *This Is the Day*

In *More Than a White Man's Religion*, my dear friend Abdu Murray has given us a timely, compelling, thought-provoking, and very helpful resource. He more than delivers when he explains why the gospel has never been white, male-centered, or just another religion. Most importantly, this book is anchored in the Scriptures and tethered to the heart and character of Jesus. As you read through these pages, you will encounter clarity and hope, but you will also be struck by the realization that Jesus is indeed refreshingly contrary to the messes we have made. Thank you, Abdu, for this gift.

DR. CRAWFORD W. LORITTS JR., author, speaker, radio host and president, Beyond our Generation

It seems that fewer people today care whether Christianity is true than care whether it is good. In this important book, Abdu Murray clearly shows that Christianity is indeed good—in fact, much better than a mere religion. Along the way he skillfully explodes the modern myths that Christianity promotes sexism and racism and then directs us back to the person of Christ. *More Than a White Man's Religion* will not allow the noise of the world to drown out the Word of God. Highly recommended.

FRANK TUREK, author and speaker, CrossExamined.org

People's perceptions are clouded concerning Christianity—often seeing it as a rules-oriented religion with limited access to certain kinds of people. In *More Than a White Man's Religion*, Abdu Murray pierces these myths and helps us grasp the staggering significance of the Bible's teachings about these vital matters, including Paul's words in Galatians 3:28: "There is neither Jew nor Gentile, neither slave nor free, nor is there male and female, for you are all one in Christ Jesus." This is a timely and important book.

MARK MITTELBERG, author of *Contagious Faith* and *The Questions Christians Hope No One Will Ask (with Answers)*

Once again Abdu Murray has provided us with a much-needed resource for addressing the seemingly insurmountable societal tensions of our day. This is an essential volume for a generation who questions if Christianity is good for people who are marginalized all too often in our society. Abdu writes with a rare blend of humility and brilliance, all while reminding us that the gospel is still and has always been good news for women (and men), ethnic minorities (and majority culture), and for those whose souls are longing for a robust relational faith that is far more than mere religion.

CHRIS BROOKS, author of *Urban Apologetics*

MORE THAN A

WHITE
MAN'S
RELIGION

MORE THAN A

WHITE
MAN'S
RELIGION

*Why the Gospel Has Never Been
Merely White, Male-Centered, or
Just Another Religion*

ABDU MURRAY

ZONDERVAN REFLECTIVE

More Than a White Man's Religion
Copyright © 2022 by Abdu Murray

Requests for information should be addressed to:
Zondervan, *3900 Sparks Dr. SE, Grand Rapids, Michigan 49546*

Zondervan titles may be purchased in bulk for educational, business, fundraising, or sales promotional use. For information, please email SpecialMarkets@Zondervan.com.

ISBN 978-0-310-14161-7 (softcover)
ISBN 978-0-310-11176-4 (audio)

Library of Congress Cataloging-in-Publication Data
Names: Murray, Abdu, author.
Title: More than a white man's religion : why the gospel has never been merely white, male-centered, or just another religion / Abdu H. Murray.
Description: Grand Rapids : Zondervan, 2022.
Identifiers: LCCN 2022013402 (print) | LCCN 2022013403 (ebook) | ISBN 9780310590064 (hardcover) | ISBN 9780310590071 (ebook)
Subjects: LCSH: Church--Catholicity. | Ethnicity--Religious aspects--Christianity. | Christianity and culture. | Jesus Christ--Example. | Christians, White. | BISAC: RELIGION / Christian Ministry / Evangelism | RELIGION / Christian Living / Social Issues
Classification: LCC BV601.3 .M87 2022 (print) | LCC BV601.3 (ebook) | DDC 262/.72--dc23/ eng/20220512
LC record available at https://lccn.loc.gov/2022013402
LC ebook record available at https://lccn.loc.gov/2022013403

Jeanne Murray Walker, "Staying Power," in *New Tracks, Night Falling* © 2009. Wm. B. Eerdmans Publishing Company, Grand Rapids, MI. Reprinted by permission of the publisher; all rights reserved.

All Scripture quotations, unless otherwise indicated, are taken from the ESV® Bible (The Holy Bible, English Standard Version®). Copyright © 2001 by Crossway, a publishing ministry of Good News Publishers. Used by permission. All rights reserved. · Scripture quotations marked NASB are taken from the New American Standard Bible®. Copyright © 1960, 1962, 1963, 1968, 1971, 1972, 1973, 1975, 1977, 1995, 2020 by The Lockman Foundation. Used by permission. www.Lockman. org. · Scripture quotations marked NIV are taken from the Holy Bible, New International Version®, NIV®. Copyright © 1973, 1978, 1984, 2011 by Biblica, Inc.® Used by permission of Zondervan. All rights reserved worldwide. www.Zondervan.com. The "NIV" and "New International Version" are trademarks registered in the United States Patent and Trademark Office by Biblica, Inc.® · The Scripture quotations marked NRSV are taken from the New Revised Standard Version Bible. Copyright © 1989 National Council of the Churches of Christ in the United States of America. Used by permission. All rights reserved worldwide.

Published in association with the literary agency of Wolgemuth & Associates, Inc.

Cover design: Brian Bobel
Cover art: © Hramikona / Shutterstock
Interior design: Sara Colley

Printed in the United States of America

HB 08.16.2023

For my daughters, whose spirits widen and deepen my appreciation for the Savior who values all women

and

For Christopher Brooks and Brandon Cleaver: Friends who have nurtured my mind with wisdom born from graciously endured hard knocks

May all of your futures be bettered when the culture looks to and looks more like Jesus, the essential value giver.

CONTENTS

CONTENTS

PREFACE

A common and understandable misconception is that an author has mastered the topic he or she has written an entire book about. That may be true for some subjects and some authors, perhaps for mathematics, elementary physics, or even history. But most topics, especially those dealing with cultural, moral, and spiritual matters, are never truly mastered, no matter how many academic degrees or experiences a person has amassed. As one who has written on such topics, I can say with paradoxical confidence that authors find their self-confidence challenged by the topics about which they write. Each topic spurs the author to self-reflect, then potentially see and confront their blind spots and shortcomings as they struggle to live consistently with their written thoughts. Indeed, I have spent days contemplating and praying even about this short preface because it speaks briefly about my own self-discovery on the journey of writing what you are about to read.

In a profoundly ironic convergence, I finished the chapters about the Bible, Jesus, and the value of women two days after the ministry of which I was once a part—Ravi Zacharias International

Ministries (RZIM)—released the report of an independent investigation it commissioned that exposed its namesake's abuses of women. The months leading up to that report, months I spent researching and writing this book, were among the most gut-twisting and heartrending of my life.

The contrarieties were dizzying. Ravi had been something of a pioneer in the world of apologetics. Decades ago, he started hiring women not only to speak on behalf of his ministry but also to lead aspects of it at a time when women apologists were exceedingly rare and sorely needed. In various settings, I've shared some of the lessons I had been learning from my experience. One such lesson is that we must be ever vigilant, aware of our ability to overlook and even blame the vulnerable or the oppressed no matter how many times we've championed their causes in the past. I had initially disbelieved and denied previous accusations about Ravi's abuse and treatment of women. I defended and repeated his denials. I continued to disbelieve, defend, and deny even after new but different accusations were brought several years later. But as more evidence mounted in 2020 and 2021, I came to believe and accept the ugly truth about what Ravi had done. During that time, I was writing this book and asking myself if I had been walking in step with Jesus—the one I follow and the one on whom this book focuses.

The difficult answer I have wrestled out of myself through prayer and tears is this: *not always.* That may sound like a trite or even exculpatory answer, but I assure you it is not. We all like to think of ourselves as pillars of consistency in our pursuits of truth and justice. But that just isn't so. We have peaks of triumph and courage but also valleys of failure and cowardice. That is the human condition. And it is my condition. But that gives me no cause to excuse myself. In fact, my confession is that I should have done better in recognizing the truth and listening to the voices of the vulnerable.

Coming to grips with my failure was particularly difficult because I have had the profound privilege of walking alongside someone who survived years of sexual abuse from early childhood and was trafficked until her late teens. Despite being robbed of her innocence, her will to trust, and her sense of safety, she found and trusted Christ as an adult. In doing so, she found herself. I met Tara before I had joined RZIM when she applied for a part-time position as my ministry assistant. She had no professional office experience. Tara eventually shared some of her story, which explained why she lacked the experience one would have expected to see. But her eagerness to learn and serve the Lord was obvious. In my legal career, I've had various assistants and can truthfully say that she has blossomed to become one of the most professionally capable assistants with whom I have had the privilege of serving. My wife, children, and friends have all been blessed by the opportunity to walk with her as the traumas of past experiences have resurfaced, bringing new waves of challenges, and by God's grace, more victory. Along the way, she has taught us far more than we have ever taught her. In fact, in the pages that follow, you will be blessed by some of her story, which she has graciously permitted me to share. Her story is not mine to tell. She tells it herself—and quite powerfully.[1]

Despite my lengthy experience walking with an abuse survivor, I failed to respond well when other women claimed to have had their vulnerabilities exploited by someone in power, someone whom I trusted and thought I knew. I could excuse my failure by arguing that the man's reputation had been sterling or that it was natural to give him the benefit of the doubt. But the truth is that while Ravi deceived me, for a time I remained willing to believe his deceptions in the face of contradicting evidence. I have not written this book about the Bible's care for the vulnerable *as* someone who has an unblemished record of listening to the vulnerable and unerringly helping them. Nor have I written this book *for* those with unblemished records. I have written it *as* a blemished person *for* blemished people.

What a contrast we are to Jesus. I have been asked to reflect on any theological lessons I had learned from that experience. I continue to learn new lessons as time passes, but more than anything I have come to greatly appreciate how Jesus—whom the Bible describes as the most powerful person ever to walk the earth—regarded the vulnerable with perfect consistency. Abuse counselor and author Diane Langberg says it well: "I have been struck by how often we are told that Jesus saw."[2] He saw the abused and those vulnerable to abuse as needing care and protection. Yet he also saw abusers of power, like Zacchaeus—who tried to hide from sight—as those needing correction, restoration, and redemption (Luke 19:1–10).[3] Jesus was consistently powerful in his vulnerability. What love-driven strength it must have taken to lay aside his power to justifiably condemn us for our sin so that he could be vulnerable on that cross on our behalf and save us. I have not written this book solely because I think others need to read it. I have written as one who needs to read it too. I continue to learn, self-reflect, and try to follow in Christ's footsteps. I hope that I can contribute something of value, especially to those who, like me, have championed the cause of the vulnerable but also unwittingly defended the powerful.

There is hope for us all, as blemished as we are, if we look to Christ, the spotless, unblemished Lamb, who through his life, death, and resurrection, set aside his power to save broken humanity. As we explore the topics of racism, sexism, equality, and the

Bible, I hope that I make the case that Jesus' character is our paradigm for progress. I am not that paradigm. But Christ is steadfast, and I hope to show this in the pages that follow. I pray that each of us—that I—imitate him better in the days that follow.

Kyrie eleison.

ABDU MURRAY
September 13, 2021

CHAPTER I

SEEING THE
SOCIAL SURGE

As I awaited my connecting flight in a New Delhi airport lounge, I found myself swimming in the mental soup that long-haul flights and jet lag so effectively plunge a person into. I was aware of my surroundings just enough to keep myself out of trouble. The cottony feeling in my head allowed for only three instincts: drink water, keep track of the time, and stare blankly.

Somehow my blank stare turned into something resembling focused attention when the television caught my eye. It showed a documentary about commuter trains that run from rural Indian villages to major cities. The program wasn't about the trains per se but rather the flood of people struggling to board them just to get to work or get home. In desperate attempts to secure a spot on the dangerously small and all-too-infrequent train cars, a river of humanity would surge into the trains at each stop. Those not fortunate enough to sardine themselves inside (if such a condition could be called fortunate) either had to wait for the next train or try something drastic to get on the train.

A disturbingly high number of people opted for drastic. At every stop, people would climb onto a train's roof and then ride there without any safety harness. People would die on those deadly commutes. But the necessity of earning a day's wage to fill the aching stomachs of children was worth the risk.

The surge of passengers getting on and off the trains were rivers of humanity too strong to resist. The program highlighted this in both tragic and comedic ways. Occasionally someone would try to get off at a particular stop, only to be thwarted by the surge of those trying to get on the train. These poor souls would be forced back into the train car only to battle even more bodies at the next stop, which might be up to an hour away from where they wanted to go. One man heroically but futilely tried to swim against the surge for multiple stops, only to find himself half a day's journey from where he was trying to be.

Social surges within a culture operate much the same way. Today, Western society rushes to board a train headed away from Christianity—especially evangelical Christianity—believing that it supports social evils like racism, sexism, and judgmentalism. Resisting that social surge seems just as futile as the efforts of that unfortunate Indian man trying to get off at his desired stop. But it isn't futile, no matter how many people are trying to board the train, especially if it is going in the wrong direction. Yes, the train away from Christianity is filling up with those who think Christianity is racist, sexist, and full of hypocrites. That trend is becoming so popular that people are not only risking themselves to get *into* the train cars, but they are climbing *on top* just to get a seat. But should we be so eager to get on a train that may be headed in the wrong direction? It may be headed away from the only worldview that dignifies all human beings.

WHY RESIST?

Of course, we would like the luxury of pausing to consider whether the social surge is pushing us onto the right train. But that's the problem with social surges, especially the modern variety: they are not only powerful but are fast and unceasing. They don't allow for careful contemplation. It's reasonable to sincerely consider the possibility that Christianity is racist, sexist, and judgmental. For two thousand years, hasn't Christianity shown itself to be a white, imperialistic religion that has enslaved people of color and established a patriarchy that oppresses women? Haven't evangelicals been hyperjudgmental about marriage and sex only to find themselves divorcing, having affairs, and watching pornography nearly as much as everyone else?

The social surge doesn't allow us to ask such questions methodically. Rather, it forces us to answer yes to all of them immediately. That immediacy is one of the chief reasons to resist the surge, even if only to ask ourselves whether we should get on or stay on the train it's pushing us toward. Pausing to give that question careful consideration allows us to test the validity of the mob's push. It must be a measured resistance, however. After all, when it comes to racism, sexism, and hypocrisy, the church's track record isn't sterling or beyond reproach. We simply cannot—we must not— ignore the wrongs of the past or the shortcomings of our present just for the sake of resistance or stubborn pride. Indeed, the Christian worldview's strength is that it acknowledges its adherents' faults and failures while pointing us all to its faultless and failure-free founder. Put simply, the gospel message is sturdy enough for us to test its mettle.

A reasoned resistance also affords us the chance to see that racism, sexism, and hypocrisy aren't just problems confronting Christianity. All of us, with whatever worldview we hold, must look into the mirrors of our lives to see where we have fallen short. One can easily document racist and sexist actions and ideas emanating from people of every major religion and from those claiming no religious beliefs. In fact, I'd venture to say that most people have acted with prejudice to some degree or have at least shown indifferent to prejudice. I'd go even further (without any real risk of being wrong) and assert that all of us have been judgmental, knowing that we'd fail to meet the same moral standards by which we've judged others.

Resisting the social surge against Christianity need not be motivated by defensiveness. Christendom's history hasn't been anywhere near perfect, but it has been unbalanced—tipped far more in favor of the good that it has done the world than the bad it has wrought. Many of the moral presuppositions with which we judge Christianity's failings arose from Christianity's victories over the immoral world in which it was birthed.[1] Failure to accurately diagnose the root causes of the social ills that beset us would be especially harmful—perhaps even socially fatal—if we mislabeled as poison one of the medications that could actually lead to the cure. I think Christianity—more specifically the Bible—has been so mislabeled.

The real strength allowing us to resist the social surge to label Christianity as racist, sexist, and judgmental has less to do with explaining away how people have manipulated the gospel message and much more to do with understanding and following the character and teaching of the person at the gospel message's heart. The gospel message runs from Genesis, the Bible's first book, to Revelation, its very last. It is my contention that where we have seen racism, misogyny, and hypocrisy in history, they have come from hearts and minds acting inconsistently with that gospel message and the example of Jesus—the one who makes the gospel "good news," which is what the word *gospel* means.

It's quite true that the credibility of the message is always judged by the integrity of the messenger. The messengers and ministers who followed Jesus didn't have impeccable integrity. Those who have made positive impacts on human history have done so inconsistently, sometimes shockingly so when it comes to matters of race and gender. Focusing on that checkered, all-too-human history blinds us from seeing Jesus' true message that God wants a relationship with every human being equally, across racial, ethnic, and gender lines.

The easy-to-make-but-hard-to-sustain accusation that the Bible condones slavery, xenophobia, and misogyny is the fuel that hurtles the train away from Christianity and foments enthusiasm in the crowds rushing to get on it. But it's a tainted fuel, no matter how much momentum the train it powers seems to have gained. That train will sputter to a halt as we make a sincere assessment of the Bible, Jesus' life, and the effects both have had on this world. At the very least, some passengers may be persuaded to resist the social surge and change trains.

In many parts of the world outside the West, there is a train gaining momentum in the other direction—toward a full embrace of the Christian message of equality and hope. That train is full of passengers from the global South and Africa, India, and parts of the Middle East who look to the life of Jesus and the hope he brings as the great equalizer and the one who dignifies all humanity. It's fascinating that non-Western people of color, both men and women, are surging to get on the very train that white Westerners claim leads to oppression.

WHY ME?

Bright, wonderful voices from within the African American and South African community have addressed the issue of racism and the Bible. Likewise, equally bright and wonderful female voices have tackled sexism and the Bible. So why would I take up writing on these subjects? What can I possibly contribute? I'm a Middle Eastern man who came to faith in Christ from a Muslim background.[2] My current experiences as an ethnic minority and my former experiences as a religious minority have afforded me a window into the perspectives of those who have experienced marginalization. Similarly, my olive skin is often mistaken for European, and so I've been granted some inclusion into the perspectives of white America. As a Middle Easterner born and raised in the United States, I've seen my male-dominated ethnicity sometimes clash with the increasingly gender sensitive Western world. Consciously or unconsciously, *we* consider *our* culture's perspective to be *the* perspective, while others' perspectives are myopic, limited, or biased. As one with an insider-outsider perspective on ethnicity, gender, and religion, I hope to contribute in a way that points to a message none of us can take credit for but each of us can own—the message that all are and should be treated as equals.

Another way in which I'm an insider colors the thoughts in the pages that follow. While I don't pretend to have endured anything close to the kind of racial prejudices others have, I have been given a glimpse of what it means to be part of a community made to feel uncomfortable due to skin tone and ethnicity. An incident from a while back comes to mind. As an attorney, I had to fly to a business meeting with a client and some business associates. I met one such associate at the gate before getting on the same flight. Though we communicated regularly by phone and email, we hadn't met face-to-face. Long before meeting him, I looked up his picture on his website so I could put a face to the voice. When we met, it was obvious that he hadn't done the same.

"You're Abdu?" he asked gruffly as our hands clasped in greeting. "I was expecting a short black guy."

My mystified shock was hard to mask. "Really? Why?" I asked as casually as I could.

"You know, because of your name," he shot back without hesitation. "Sometimes black guys have weird first names like yours and regular last names, you know?"

He managed to efficiently offend two ethnicities with one stone. He hadn't taken the time to look up my (easily available) photo on the internet nor to learn the ethnic origin of my name. Looking back on this incident now, I wonder how "Mr. Smith" would have reacted had he been meeting my colleague Brandon Cleaver. Would he have been just as surprised to find that, despite Brandon's "not-weird" first and last names, he's African American? It was a minor incident to be sure, but that slight sting helped sensitize me to the lashes others have felt.

I've seen the inside of what it's like to experience ethnic slurs— and I confess I've also dished them out. Like all cultures, Arab culture has a checkered past and a not-so-pristine present when it comes to race. The broad label "Arab" suggests a uniform ethnic and cultural experience. Yet it masks the reality that the Arab world is hardly uniform or united and suffers from its own internal prejudices. From the Lebanese to the Iraqis to the Yemenis to the Saudis (and everyone in between), the superficially uniform Arab world is pockmarked with its own prejudices within the Middle East and the Arab diaspora. As an aside, this shows that white people don't have the monopoly on ethnic disparagement. Ibram Kendi, for example, recounts how African Americans he knew growing up would look with disdain on black people who emigrated to the United States from Africa or the Caribbean.[3] Ask any Indian about the animus between southern and northern Indians, between darker and lighter complected Indians. Yes, my culture—whether it be my Arab culture or my American culture—is just as littered with racism and ethnic animus as any other.

Allow just one more example of what I've seen when it comes to race and ethnicity. The commonly used word by some Arabs to refer to black people is *abid*. *Abid* does not mean black. The Arabic word for black is *sood* or *aswad*. In fact, *abid* does not refer to color at all. It literally means *slave* or *servant*. My given name—Abdu—derives from the same Arabic word for slave. My name literally means "His [God's] slave" and is an honorable name meant to highlight one's religious devotion. I've thought about that juxtaposition for years, how giving someone a name like Abdu is meant as a compliment, yet calling a person of a different race an *abid* is a veiled insult. A moment's reflection here is critical. My name—the way I'm identified to the world—can fuel Arabic racial slurs and spur my white former business colleague's stereotypical misidentification of me as black. I have seen racial insults served with a side of french fries and a side of hummus. The human cross-cultural capacity to denigrate that which is inherently honorable is fascinating indeed. This is the experience from which I see the racial issues we face in our day. This is the experience from which I have seen Jesus as refreshingly contrary to the messes we have made.

Something similar is at work regarding my perspectives on the plight of women today and the role of Christianity in addressing that plight. Patriarchal and misogynistic thinking has troubled Middle Eastern culture for centuries. And yet it is that same culture from which I learned to honor my family's matriarchs for their value, virtue, and authority. Their examples taught me to look at women with respect, although I've done so imperfectly. Such an imperfect episode happened a few years ago. At an open forum at a university in California, I was engaging with a young woman who had a very fiery personality. During the Q&A, she took issue with something I said during my main address. As we talked after the event, several bystanders joined our conversation. Though this was not the topic of our conversation, I recall thinking of how Jesus thoughtfully engaged with women on tough issues even though it was culturally taboo for those women to approach a man that way. With her sharp and informed mind, the young woman I was conversing with certainly hadn't been intimidated by a man. I thought our lively conversation was going well, even if we didn't agree on the matter at hand. But I failed to notice something that Jesus would have picked up on. Despite her obvious pluck, she spoke with such a low volume that I had trouble hearing her in the echoey room. I repeatedly stepped toward her and leaned in to try to hear what she was saying. I hadn't noticed that she kept stepping back. Finally, she had to ask me to "stop looming" because it was making her uncomfortable. She (like most people) was considerably shorter than me. I was just trying to hear her better, but she thought I was taking an aggressive posture. I explained myself to her, but it occurred to me that she might have felt uncomfortable because of similar tactics other men may have used to intimidate her in conversations. She wasn't intimidated by me, but she wasn't comfortable either. You see, I wasn't wrong to try to hear her—that was the honoring thing to do. Ironically, while I had succeeded in hearing her words, I had failed to read her signals about the dynamics of our conversation.

I've been blessed to be married to a woman of exceptional gifts and strengths. Her tenacity and grit rival that of any man I've ever met. My daughters exhibit strength, character, and faith that I'm sure flow from my wife's example. Like so many people, I have encountered mixed messages about gender equality and relations. Yet I found myself marrying an equal who partners with me in raising two women who are no less than our son's equal. It is our hope to raise a son who sees himself as no greater nor any less than the women he has the privilege of encountering. I was raised to honor women, and I was blessed with wonderful exemplars growing up. Yet the cultures of which I am a product, both Western and Middle Eastern, are only now learning to deal with a prolonged record of misogyny. This insider/outsider position in which I find myself compels me to share something about how the Christian message—a message I once thought was wanting—can contribute to the solutions we desperately need. Jesus, as God taking on human form and entering our sin-lousy world, is an insider/outsider as well. It is not lost on me that perhaps my own insider/outsider background impels me to see Jesus as one whose example of valuing women of every stripe and strata is worthy of our attention.

WHY NOW?

Even as I write, a Vesuvius of outrage over claims of racial injustice is erupting all over the world following the death of unarmed African American George Floyd during an arrest. His death follows a series of deaths of unarmed African Americans that have pressurized the magma flowing beneath society's crust. At the heart of it all is a growing belief that white evangelicalism is at least partially to blame. And if white evangelicalism is to blame, maybe the Christian message itself is to blame. Perhaps these thoughts have been building for years only now to erupt into a full-blown movement that sees itself righteously opposed to the Christian message. Perhaps not, considering that some Christians are also involved in the movement. I won't pretend to provide a solution to our social ills, nor will I attempt to address the political movements behind all of this. My aim, humbly, is to show that the gospel message is the wrong target of our collective outrage because it may be the solution to the very ills for which it is blamed.

With the rise of the #MeToo movement, we have witnessed a swell in women reporting demeaning and harassing conduct in various settings—from boardrooms to Hollywood sets to university athletic departments to religious institutions. Director Harvey Weinstein and others have not only been called to account professionally but also have been brought to justice judicially. Still, so many women endure overt sexism or the subtler varieties (being called "sweetheart" by managers or feeling a hand at the small of the back are just two examples of many). No area of culture is immune from this disease. Sexual discrimination and misogyny (even abuse) from within church leadership is being brought to the light of day. I recently lived through a horrific discovery of such abuse by a leader I greatly respected. This issue is everywhere and crosses political and social lines. Despite the universal infection of racism and sexism, somehow evangelical Christianity has become the chief antagonist in the cultural controversies. While the vilification of Christianity is factually wrong, we are awash in a post-truth world in which facts get in the way of feelings and feelings have more persuasive power than ever before. And, to be fair, Christians themselves have not always behaved in ways that correct the misperception and have, unfortunately, fostered it.

It didn't take the rise of such movements for most to realize that pressure has been increasing over the issues of racial and gender equality and Christianity's influence. I have spent a lot of time speaking at secular universities and other gatherings, addressing questions that hit hard at the foundations of the Christian faith. In years past, those questions centered largely on factual and philosophical matters: *What evidence is there that Jesus rose from the dead bodily? If an all-powerful, all-loving God exists, why is there so much suffering and evil in the world?* A seismic shift has taken place in the past decade, however. The most common questions now revolve around social issues and the perceived evils of religion, particularly Christianity. In fact, the questions are usually worded not in terms of genuine inquiries but in terms that assume Christianity's failings. *Isn't the Bible a misogynistic book that supports an oppressive patriarchy? Doesn't the Bible condone slavery, tribalism, and ethnic cleansing? Shouldn't we look to any source other than Christianity to direct our moral compasses? How can Christ be the solution when Christians seem to be the problem?* The overarching pathos of these questions is not factual—it is moral and visceral. They smack of an attorney cross-examining a hostile witness.

WHY JESUS?

Yet such questions cannot be answered apart from facts and data coupled with compassion and moral clarity. In light of the movements that have turned their sights on Christianity, addressing whether Jesus has anything of contemporary value to teach us is critical in this cultural moment.

These are matters of justice, after all, and the Bible is concerned, perhaps even obsessed, with justice (the word *justice* or some derivation thereof is used hundreds of times in the Bible). Inspired by the Bible, Martin Luther King Jr. led one of the most influential civil justice movements in modern times. While in jail for pursuing justice, King famously wrote, "Injustice anywhere is a threat to justice everywhere. We are caught in an inescapable network of mutuality, tied in a single garment of destiny. Whatever affects one directly, affects all indirectly."[4] His profound comment just as easily applies to both gender discrimination and moral hypocrisy.

It's ironic that Dr. King's statement is anchored in his belief in God, yet the social surge pushes us onto the train speeding away from the Bible that inspired King. The irony, I believe, is that the biblical message is the only message that actually legitimizes our pursuit of racial justice and gender equality because it is the only message that legitimizes the very concepts of justice and equality in the first place. This isn't to say that non-Christians don't have a sense of justice or equality or haven't pursued them. The Bible tells us that all people—regardless of their faith or nonfaith—have a sense of right and wrong inscribed on their hearts (Rom. 2:15). It comes as no surprise, therefore, that non-Christians have successfully pursued justice and have righted inequities. Yet God, as described in the Bible, is the grounding of all justice and human dignity. It is God who directs us to "act justly and to love mercy and to walk humbly with your God" (Mic. 6:8 NIV) and who grounds the very concepts of justice, mercy, and humility. I hope to defend the claim that we mustn't get on the train that leads away from that message.

Whether we sincerely consider that claim depends largely on the blind spots with which we live. Anthony B. Bradley has edited a powerful book on ethnicity and the Bible based on leveling our moral playing fields. In his contribution, Bradley explains that we all have blind spots when it comes to race and ethnicity, and that we often cling to narratives that either downplay our roles in perpetuating injustice or exaggerate our efforts at eradicating injustice. Bradley uses the evangelical tendency to idealize the Puritans as an example of such blind spots because among the Puritans were slave owners.[5]

Blind spot seems too trivial a word to describe racism, slavery, and sexism, doesn't it? How can some of the worst injustices in human history be mere blind spots? The word is quite apt, actually, because blind spots aren't merely oversights. If unchecked, blind spots can lead to disaster. As of this writing, my fifteen-year-old daughter is just beginning to drive, which means that my wife and I have obsessively talked to her about blind spots. As the father of a newly minted driver, I can assure you that blind spots are anything but trivial. When a motorcycle or a bicyclist is in a driver's blind spot, failure to check it won't just result in a bent fender. It will result in tragedy. Likewise, race, gender, and hypocrisy aren't trivial matters. We would do well to pay attention to whether we have a blind spot when it comes to our views of the Christian message, lest tragedies should pile up.

Our blind spots enlarge when we turn allies into foes, a skill at which we are becoming alarmingly adept. The "Christian Revolution," as Tom Holland has called it, is responsible for so much of what is good in society.[6] The Christian message inspired Christians to construct hospitals and establish universities. The message inspired the abolitionists and those who opposed apartheid. Yet today the Christian message is viewed with moral suspicion. And now a growing blind spot in culture obscures the Christian message's beneficence and transforms it into malevolence.

Consider this contrast. Some years ago, well-known conservative radio host Dennis Prager debated atheist Oxford professor Jonathan Glover on God's existence. The cross-fire segment of formal debates in which the debaters ask each other tough questions is usually where debates are won. To make the point that the Bible is good for society, Prager asked Professor Glover to imagine a situation in which his car broke down in the middle of the night in a rough area of Los Angeles (this was before the ubiquity of mobile phones, making a walk to a pay phone more likely). "If, as you stepped out of the car with fear and trembling," Prager asked, "you were suddenly to hear the weight of pounding footsteps behind you, and you saw ten burly young men who had just stepped out of a dwelling coming toward you, would it or would it not make a difference to you to know that they were coming from a Bible study?"[7] The rhetorical point was obvious.

That question would likely backfire in today's climate. You see, a clever opponent who understands which train society is surging to get on would have a snappy, equally powerful comeback. "Yes," he might say. "I'd be terrified if I was black, a woman, transgender, or gay."

Christianity and Christians were once the dragon slayers. Now they are the imagined dragons whose breath is the fire of racism, sexism, and hypocritical judgment. But we must be careful here: Christendom, as a social construction of people calling themselves Christians, has had its pockmarked history of racism, misogyny, and social ills. This must be addressed and dealt with as part of the vigilance I mentioned above. Undue vilification of Christianity as a set of propositional claims, however, is something we must also be vigilant about. There remain real battles to fight and real dragons to slay when it comes to racism, misogyny, and judgmentalism. I fear we may never slay them if we transform the Christian message from the dove meant to bring "peace on earth, and goodwill toward men" into the dragon of a white, male-centered, superstitious religion.

In his book *The Madness of Crowds*, secular writer Douglas Murray argues that we find foes around every corner and get offended at the slightest provocation because we lack meaning in our lives, and imagining dragons fills that meaning-shaped void. He urges us to find meaning by cultivating our relationships, striving for mutual respect amid disagreement, and finding personal fulfillment instead of manufacturing new battles to fight. He offers us another train to board—the train of personal fulfillment and mutual respect.[8] But isn't the basis of the problem that human beings tend away from those things, not toward them? No matter how appealing that train may seem to be, it is just on a loop, like a toy train that takes its passengers right back to where they started. Part of the human condition is to seek fulfillment by vilifying others. We tend to focus on ourselves and those like us. Secular solutions ultimately proceed in a circle because they don't understand the starting point of the human condition nor the destination. Jesus' message contrasts like a blood stain on new snow. He tells us that the human heart is the heart of the problem (Matt. 15:19). That kind of stark realism is worth listening to or at least considering. Yet God has not left us to our condition (John 3:16; Rom. 5:8; 2 Cor. 5:17). Seeing if that train can get us to where we need to be is worth resisting the cultural surge. That train is pulling up to our stop. Let us resist the surge for at least a moment to see where the train might take us.

This isn't to say that common belief will make our problems vanish. History has shown us that common belief isn't a sufficient condition for social change. I hope to defend, however, that it is a necessary condition. Truly understanding what that belief actually is based on can tell us whether to stay on the train in which we find ourselves or to resist the social surge for just long enough to see if the train headed toward the gospel message might orient us to the right direction.

CHAPTER 2

DEFINING THE OBJECTION

S ome years ago, I had the privilege of chatting over good pizza and lots of cola with a thoughtful and creative young African American man. He was raised in a family professing faith in Christ, but someone he had grown close to exposed him to arguments that denounced Christianity as the means by which slavers of old had baptized their trade, and that modern racists have justified policies that hurt African Americans. The young man gave ear to these accusations, and he, too, came to view Christianity as the inherently racist "white man's religion." For various other reasons, he eventually gave up belief in God altogether.

We found ourselves engaging in philosophy and gorging on pizza (to be candid, I was gorging while he, consistent with his slender frame, ate a couple of slices). Soon into the conversation, the young man brought up his accusation that the Bible is inherently racist. The incendiary topic didn't prevent him from being cordial even as he didn't pull his rhetorical punches. In fact, it was one of the most pleasant conversations I've had about such an unpleasant matter. Politely yet passionately, he started with Old Testament passages that he believed condoned slavery and ended with his claim that in the New Testament, neither Jesus nor the apostle Paul condemned the practice. While Christianity was his main target, the young man considered religious belief in general to foster a tribalism that pits different people groups against each other and inevitably results in racial prejudice. Though it wasn't the main topic of conversation, he also claimed that the Bible treats women as subordinate to men. With all of that, he had enough reason to disqualify Christianity as a racist, sexist, white man's religion.

WHAT EXACTLY IS A "WHITE MAN'S" RELIGION?

Our conversation went surprisingly well. As with most such discussions, however, I experienced the "coulda, shoulda, wouldas"—the nagging regret that comes with thinking of something better to say or more insightful to ask hours after a conversation has ended. One question I wish I would have asked him is this: *What does it mean to claim that Christianity is a white man's religion?* From my experience as a litigator, getting clarity about the claims being made by or against my clients in court was imperative. Indeed, due process of law demands such clarity because without knowing exactly what an accusation means, the accused is robbed of the opportunity to properly defend himself. If we are to put Christianity on trial for being a white man's religion, we had better know what we mean by that claim.

To highlight the nuance needed to address the accusation, let's consider a different question I'm frequently asked due to my background. As a former Muslim, I'm frequently asked whether Islam is a religion of peace. It's a reasonable question, given two contrasting experiences in our contemporary world. When Islam dominates the headlines, it's usually because of some act of violence. Yet the vast majority of Muslims are not crouching behind airport stairwells, twisting their mustaches and thinking of ways to blow up the place. Indeed, many of us know Muslims who are among the most genuine, warmhearted people we've ever met and who contribute wonderfully to society. So we understandably try to reconcile the competing perceptions about Islam as a religion and Muslims as people. The question is straightforwardly asked, but its implications are nuanced.

The answer must, therefore, be nuanced. "It depends," I usually respond (typical for a lawyer, I know). "It depends on what one means by 'religion' and on what one means by 'peace.'" Sifting through the nuances not only supplies clarity but also exposes the motivations behind the question. Does one ask this question to get information that will assist in understanding the contrary pictures of Islam we get? Or is one really making a statement in the form of a question, an attempt to get validation for a predrawn conclusion that Islam and Muslims are as bad as the questioner already believes them to be? It does, indeed, depend on what one means by religion. If, by religion, we mean the doctrines and tenets of a faith as set forth in the sacred texts and life of the religion's founder, we will get one answer. If, by religion, we mean the beliefs and actions of the vast majority of those who seriously claim to be Muslim, we may get another answer altogether. You see, human history and our contemporary experience teach us that there is often a gap between what a religious system teaches and what its adherents actually believe and do.

Why bring up Islam when Christianity is at issue here? Because it's critical to bring similar nuance to determine whether Christianity is a white man's religion. Do we ask this question to get a true, fact-based understanding of Christianity's teachings and the behavioral templates to be drawn from Jesus' life? Or is this really just an accusation disguised as a question? I fear that some make the charge against Christianity without giving much thought to what it means beyond its rhetorical power to shut down discussion. Uncovering the true motive is key to uncovering what the accusation means and whether any answer would satisfy us. We can never answer whether Christianity is a white man's religion until we answer why we've asked in the first place.

The motivation behind answering the question is just as important as the motivation behind asking it. Confirmation bias—every person's tendency to interpret the evidence in a way that favors one's view—is something with which we each must wrestle. Does the Christian rationalize away difficult passages of the Bible or gloss over awful periods of Christian history? Does the critic interpret biblical passages in the most uncharitable light possible and ignore all the good that Christians have done for racial justice and gender equality? We can never answer the question at hand until we answer the question of our hearts.

So what does it mean for Christianity—or any religion for that matter—to be *white* or *male*? Obviously, this isn't to claim that Christianity has its own racial or gender identity, just as concepts like logic or math don't have their own ethnicities or genders. People have ethnicities; ideas do not. So when we ask whether Christianity is a white man's religion, do we mean that most Christians are white males or that its most influential members are white men? Do we mean that its doctrines and ideas appeal mostly to white men like, say, music by Kenny Rogers or even Kid Rock? Do we mean that Christianity was founded by white people? Or do we mean that white people have used Christianity to control other ethnicities? Perhaps one might be tempted to answer, "All of the above." Such a sweeping statement would be in keeping with the current social surge. But would it be accurate and even helpful?

WAS CHRISTIANITY FOUNDED BY WHITE MEN?

I'm struck by how often Western movies and television programs depict Jesus, his disciples, and the prophets of the Old Testament as if they were Europeans. Perhaps the reason is as innocuous as the fact that the pool of available actors is populated with mostly white Westerners. Perhaps the reason is that Western film and television producers (and their audiences) subconsciously project their own images onto the heroes we depict. Of late, however, the issue has become more than a matter of curiosity. It has become a source of social upheaval. The claim is that depicting Jesus as a white, Western European is an expression of white supremacy, akin to declaring that even God thinks that white people are the superior race, given that he chose to incarnate himself as one of them. Whether that criticism has any merit isn't the point. The point is that Jesus' ethnicity and the origins of Christianity suddenly matter quite a bit.

It is beyond serious dispute that Jesus was an olive-skinned Middle Eastern Jew from the Judaean province occupied by the

Roman Empire. His original disciples were all Middle Eastern Jews. The apostle Paul, Christianity's most famous convert, was a Mediterranean Jew as well as a Roman citizen. Nearly everyone involved in Christianity's founding was from somewhere other than Western Europe.

The very first mass conversion after Jesus' resurrection is depicted as a mosaic of ethnic diversity. In the book of Acts, we read that people of at least fifteen different ethnicities visited Jerusalem for the celebration of Pentecost (Acts 2:5–11). Among this ethnically diverse crowd were Arabs, North Africans, and Romans (European ancestors). These facts alone give the lie to the idea that Christianity was incepted by white Westerners. There is more subtlety to be noticed here, however. This account includes Arabs along with Jews from Judea. Those two peoples have practically perfected the art of ethnic hostility. Yet both ethnicities were present to hear the gospel message, and both embraced it as a message that spoke to them.

That the gospel message spoke to them separately was quite literally the case. Miraculously, Jesus' disciples preached the gospel message to the various ethnic groups in the languages of those very ethnic groups despite not knowing how to speak those languages. The crowds were amazed, saying, "We hear them telling in our own tongues the mighty works of God," and asking, "What does this mean?" (Acts 2:11–12). Let's be clear: they weren't struggling to understand *what* they were hearing. They struggled to understand *why* they were hearing it in their own language. While the skeptic might scoff at the miraculous aspect of this account, the point here is that the Bible—the very book so many claim resists valuing ethnic diversity—goes out of its way to make such diversity a thing of foundational value. The fact that the disciples' message was conveyed with a unity of content through diversity of language was part of the message itself—that the gospel is good news for all people. The gospel doesn't require us to speak the same language, change our names, or ingest the same foods. The gospel does not ethnically homogenize; it spiritually unifies.

A smile parts my lips as I marinate in the reality that the God of the Bible is not tribal; he favors no one race while dignifying all ethnicities with his message. On Pentecost three thousand people—from Europe, Africa, the Middle East, and Asia—become the seedlings of the Christian church.[1]

From its birth to its adolescence, the church continued to be a tapestry of color. Within the first three centuries of nascent Christianity, North Africans were among the most influential church fathers. Tertullian, Origen, Augustine, and Athanasius were all Africans and among the most influential thinkers and theologians of Christianity's first few centuries. Tertullian often criticized Hellenistic (European) philosophy and himself greatly influenced the theology of the West. Augustine's theology and thinking would eventually have a tremendous impact on European theologians like John Calvin. African countries like Nubia and Ethiopia had embraced the Christian message without Roman rule or influence.[2] In the early days, darker skinned people were the pulse of the church and effectuated positive change in the West.

Women played (and continue to play) significant roles in the founding of Christianity. Yes, men were primarily in leadership positions, but a woman was chosen to be the vessel by which the Savior of the world would be born. Women financially supported Jesus' ministry freely and from their own monetary resources. Women had the fortitude to stay with Jesus as he was executed, and they rose early in the morning to anoint his body at his tomb. Women were given the honor of witnessing Christianity's founding miracle, the resurrection. Women flocked to Jesus and to the early church, leaving behind their former faiths or the paganism of which they were a part. By the second century, two-thirds of all Christians were women who were significantly and positively impacting the world around them despite the hardships they faced. They did this freely because at the core of Jesus' message were the dignity, significance, and equality other faiths and society at large had denied them. Michael Kruger put it succinctly: "Christianity was not mocked in the early centuries for being anti-woman. It was mocked for being so pro-women. Christianity was made fun of by the cultural elites in the Greco-Roman world because so many Christians were women. As a result, the elites said, 'Oh, this is a religion for women and children.'"[3]

I could cite many examples, but the point has been made. Indeed, it almost seems too easy to prove that Christianity was not founded by white males.

WAS CHRISTIANITY TAKEN OVER BY WHITE PEOPLE?

Perhaps, one might argue, that while Christianity wasn't started by Western European men, they quickly seized control of it. This may be what is motivating racial justice activists to decry depictions of Jesus as European looking. They claim that "white Jesus" iconography is an attempt to appropriate history's most influential figure as an icon of white superiority over and against the inferiority of brown people. When Christianity expanded primarily to the West, it eventually became the Roman Empire's official religion under Constantine, thereby making it a white, imperialistic religion.

Making the Son of God into the image of white Europeans sends a powerful message, so the criticism goes.

The problem is that this commonly believed narrative is almost entirely wrong. While Christianity's westward expansion gets a lot of attention, we miss the fact that Christianity spread into the East even more extensively. While we know *that* this happened, unfortunately we have only scant historical evidence of *how* this happened. Rodney Stark tells us, "From the earliest days, the Jesus Movement appears to have devoted its primary efforts to the East, as reflected in the rapid growth and spread of eastern Christianity, once stretching from Syria to China."[4] The fruits of that eastward expansion persist today, evidenced by significant Christian presences in the Middle East and growing Christian communities in the Far East. Even though Christians there are experiencing genocide-level persecutions, the Eastern church survives and in some places thrives. The very fact that Christian communities started and persist in so many countries utterly unaffected by Rome or Constantine is enough to show that Christianity's global influence wasn't just due to Europeans.

For a long time, the popular belief has been that the Roman emperor Constantine made Christianity the empire's state religion and then fused it with politics, military power, and world domination. History, however, reveals that after his conversion, Constantine was remarkably tolerant of non-Christian religions, even appointing pagans to high-profile political offices. Although he helped to fund church buildings and appointed Christian clergy to political positions, he never actually made Christianity Rome's official religion. Fascinatingly, Constantine was rather intolerant of dissent *within* the Christian community, often opposing those he did not think conformed to Christian orthodoxy. Paganism lived on under Constantine's rule and for some time after. Summing up Constantine's role in Christian history, Stark writes that he "was not responsible for the triumph of Christianity. By the time he gained the throne, Christian growth already had become a tidal wave of exponential increase."[5] Even after Constantine and even when the church rose once again to political prominence, "the church did not exploit its official standing to quickly stamp out paganism, nor did the emperors accomplish this on behalf of the new faith. Instead, paganism survived relatively unmolested for centuries after the conversion of Constantine, only slowly sinking into obscurity, meanwhile managing to create niches for some of its traditions within Christianity and to live on among the only slightly Christianized Europeans."[6]

What did follow, however, was not the imposition of Christianity on Easterners or Africans. Instead, quite the opposite happened. By the end of the fourteenth century, Islamic westward expansion had decimated the Christian populations in the Middle East and North Africa. Drawing from historian Philip Jenkins, Stark concludes that "Christianity became a European faith because Europe was the only 'continent where it was not destroyed.'"[7]

In the early days, Rome did not manipulate the gospel to baptize its imperialism of dark-skinned people.[8] Rather, it was the gospel that softened harsh Roman policies and politics. It is important to be clear here. Yes, in time the church—an organization run by flawed humans—became the bedfellow of power. Clergy curried favor with politicians and vice versa. The inevitable result, as seems to be the case regardless of which religion is at issue, is that the blurring of religion and politics at the organizational level distorted both. From there it was only a matter of time before selfishly ambitious people would don religious vestments to legitimize their political power grabs. Among the resultant horrors was the race-based transatlantic slave trade, which would arise centuries later. This is not something we will skirt here. Indeed, we will address it soon.

But what often gets missed is that the Christian message revolutionized so much about pagan Rome that much of modern Western civilization owes a debt to that message. Within the first two centuries of Christianity's birth, Jews were being expelled from Rome. It was Christians—themselves outcasts—who took in those Jews. It was common in Rome to view human beings in two classes: persons and nonpersons. Indeed, the English word *person* comes from the Latin word *persona*, which means "mask." We use this word today to describe when someone assumes a character artificial to their own (for example, they take on an "authoritative persona" or a "demure persona"). In other words, personhood was an artificial status conferred by the state, not by birth nor by the gods, and usually because of social standing, property ownership, or military service. This may be difficult for us to grasp today because, as David Bentley Hart notes, we use the word *person* with "a splendidly indiscriminate generosity, applying it without hesitation to everyone, regardless of social station, race, or sex."[9] We imbibe in that "splendidly indiscriminate generosity" because of Christianity's novel notion of equal personhood. Equality among people of the same race—let alone among those of different races—simply wasn't a category for the Romans. The influx of the Christian message changed that for the better. According to Hart, equality, economic and social justice, and basic human dignity weren't unfashionable in pagan, pre-Christian Rome—they were unintelligible.[10] Putting an even finer point on it, Hart writes, "It is simply the case that we distant children of the pagans would not be able to believe in any of these things—they would never have occurred to us—had our ancestors not once believed that God is love, that charity is the foundation of all virtues, that all of us are equal before the eyes of God, that to fail to feed the hungry or care for the suffering is to sin against Christ, and that Christ laid down his life for the least of his brethren."[11]

Historian Tom Holland's intellectual revolution reveals much about how veiled these historical truths—and their impacts—have been. Holland originally set out to write a book about the wonders modern civilization has inherited from the Romans. He was shocked, however, to discover that we had actually inherited our modern values not from the Roman Empire but from Christianity. He was disgusted to find that the Roman machine was "built on systematic exploitation. The entire economy is founded on slave labor. The sexual economy is founded on the absolute right of free Roman males to have sex with anyone that they want, any way that they like. And, in almost every way, this is a world that is unspeakably cruel to our way of thinking."[12] In other words, Holland discovered that the Roman Empire was a racially charged, misogynistic milieu into which Christianity was born. Holland found in the Christian message something starkly opposite to Roman ideals. The gospel was an opposing message of equality, regardless of race, sex, or status, that pushed relentlessly against the Roman social phalanx and eventually overcame inequality and brutality with dignity and compassion.[13] "Christ and Caesar had met in the arena," wrote historian Will Durant, "and Christ had won."[14]

This history pushes against the social surge that decries Christianity as the tool of white imperialists. The truth is that Christianity—the olive-skinned religion of the East that matured in North Africa—influenced white Europe, and thus all of the

West, for the better. All of the notions we cherish today—all of the notions we claim Christianity has violated—were brought into our lives by the Christian message.

THE CORE OF THE CLAIM

The question now, however, is this: *If Christianity wasn't a white man's religion historically, is it a white man's religion today?*

The answer is as fascinating as the question. We're often told that religion in general, and Christianity in particular, is dying in the West, possibly even in the world. The reality, however, is that Christianity is growing around the world. What is fascinating is where—and among whom and why—Christianity is spreading.

Christianity is growing fastest within non-white populations around the world and even within the West. We learn from Soong-Chan Rah, "Contrary to popular opinion, the church is not dying in America; it is alive and well, but it is alive and well among the immigrant and ethnic minority communities and not among the majority white churches in the United States."[15] Rodney Stark's carefully researched data on Christianity's presence around the world reveals that "Christianity is not only the largest religion in the world; it also is the least regionalized."[16] Put another way, Christianity is the least ethnically and nationally tethered religion. Put yet another way, not only is Christianity not white, it is not fettered by any ethnicity.

When we look at the data for committed Christians (those who are weekly attenders of a church), we see just how "not white" Christianity really is. According to Stark, "Christians are concentrated in Latin America (23 percent), Sub-Saharan Africa

(23 percent), and Europe (22 percent). But when the statistics are based on weekly church attenders, Europe (16 percent) falls to a distant third and Sub-Saharan Africa rises to the top (33 percent), with Latin America second (25 percent)."[17] Yes, white America is still very religious. But Christianity's growth beyond America and Europe shows that, globally speaking, it cannot seriously be called a white religion if what we mean is that most Christians are white.[18]

In Africa Christianity has been exploding in recent decades. This surge is particularly significant because it sped up since the *end* of Western colonial rule, a fact that also withstands today's social surge.[19] Lamin Sanneh puts it well: "Africa has become, or is becoming, a Christian continent in cultural as well as numerical terms, while on the same scale the West has become, or is rapidly becoming, a post-Christian society."[20] If the West is becoming less Christian while the gospel is spreading in Africa, it becomes hard to justify the claim that Christianity currently is being imposed on Africans by Western imperialists. Ironically, to make such a claim bloats Western importance beyond the facts and smacks of Western ethnocentricity. The data shows that Christianity swells in Sub-Saharan Africa not because of white missionaries, *but because of Africans.* "On the whole, missionaries no longer play a significant role in African Christianity. The extraordinary Christianization of Sub-Saharan Africa was accomplished mainly by Africans and sustained by new denominations they originated."[21]

If white colonialism really were the primary driver for Christianity's presence in Africa, Asia, and South America, we would expect it to be diminishing significantly as colonialism's grip weakens. Yet Christianity is growing in all of those areas. Perhaps the reason is that the gospel, with its Eastern origins, appeals to non-Westerners quite apart from any colonial influence.

Now, one might be tempted to argue that the non-whites have embraced Christianity because they are haunted by the postcolonial aftereffects on their psyches. To suggest this is to tread on dangerously condescending ground. First, this assumes that these poor victims of colonialism simply don't know any better to realize they are Christians only because power-driven colonizers had indoctrinated them. It's only white, Western people who have the good sense and education to be aware of why non-whites believe what they do. Such thinking is condescending at best and colonial itself at worst.

Second, the claim assumes that the attraction to Christianity is either material or political. Some argue that Christianity's growth in Latin America, for example, is due to Catholic and Protestant programs that provide material goods for those otherwise deprived. In other words, Latin Americans turned to Christianity only because missionaries met their material needs. As for the alleged political reasons, the argument goes that people convert to curry favor with the dominant, Christianity-linked political regimes influential in those areas. Both claims run afoul of actual data. First, many who convert to Christianity or who would call themselves regular churchgoers don't come from poor, materially deprived backgrounds. And those who have suffered from material deprivation often convert to Christianity without any material promises made to them. Sweeping the legs out from under the material gain argument is the fact that missionary movements infused with offers of material gain often failed.[22] Likewise, political expediency accounts for conversions even less. Christian communities are growing fastest under political regimes dominated by hostile, non-Christian ideologies. From many indications, the church is growing fastest in China (under an anti-religion political regime) and in Iran (under an Islamic political and religious regime). Being a Christian brings many consequences in such environments, and none of them includes material gain or political clout. Indeed, becoming a Christian in those areas risks and may even forfeit a person's safety. To quote Stark on this point one last time, "Churches thrive by offering an appealing faith, not by trying to buy people off with political promises."[23]

Given that Christianity exploded among women (two-thirds of all Christians in the second century were women) and continues to be popular among women today, one would be hard-pressed to argue that Christianity was imposed on them by white males. Michael Kruger recounts the story of a woman named Marcia who was the mistress of the cruel Roman emperor Commodus. She converted to Christianity while risking the ire of her merciless master. Yet she shared her faith with Commodus and influenced him to such a degree that he showed mercy to Christian prisoners.[24] Marcia is but one example of women coming to faith in Christ, not in obeisance to power but in defiance of it. We see this happening today. Reports are that the church in Iran is the fastest-growing underground church in the world despite the religious oppression there.[25] More surprising yet are the reports that the swell in the church is being led by so many women in a context where outspoken women have so much to lose.[26]

Might it be then that the gospel's expansion among non-whites and women has more to do with its substance than with its power, provision, or politics?

THE UGLY SIDE OF HISTORY

How then, if the historical and demographic facts are so clear, does one come to believe that Christianity is a white man's religion?

Having heard from Christian and non-Christian women and people of color on this question, I believe the answer lies at least partially in the fact that pain from discrimination has a way of altering perceptions and obscuring reality. Let me be clear: the discrimination and ill treatment of ethnic minorities and women has been and continues to be real. To be even clearer, some of that ill treatment has come and still comes at the hands of those claiming to be Christians. But those pain-filled facts can lead the victims and their sympathizers to hold mistake-filled perceptions about the cause of that pain.

Permit me, if you will, a lighthearted illustration to make the point about such a heavyhearted subject. For whatever reason (certainly not genetic), my kids love board games and frequently ask me to play. As a loving father does, I participate in something I dislike to bring a smile to the ones I love. A board game I dislike the least is called Googly Eyes. One player on a team draws a card and has to sketch what the card describes. His teammate has to guess what he's drawing before the sand in a small plastic hourglass runs out. The catch, though, is that the player doing the drawing has to wear a pair of glasses that grossly distorts his perception of the paper he's sketching on. Doodling a teapot under pressure is challenging enough for some even without being unable to see whether the pencil is connecting the lines or even touching the paper. The player drawing the picture knows what the card describes, yet he struggles to depict it and his teammate struggles to decipher what the sketch is supposed to represent. At some point, the situation is reversed. The player tasked with drawing what the card describes doesn't wear the googly glasses. His teammate does. The guesser has to look at a perfectly clear picture through distorting lenses to guess what was drawn.

I suspect we're trying to answer the challenge of what it means for Christianity to be a white man's religion while beset with a different kind of googly glasses. We have a hard time communicating what we mean, and we have a hard time understanding what others mean. A black person, for example, who tries to explain why she thinks Christianity is a white man's religion may struggle to put a lifetime of painful experience into words. It would be like asking a fish to describe what it means to be wet or asking a sighted person to describe the color red to someone who has never seen. Perhaps those experiences have blurred the true picture of Christianity so much that articulation becomes almost impossible. Similarly, a white Christian who is faced with the accusation may struggle to understand a perfectly clear explanation of the objection because that white person's own life distorts his ability to understand. Yet both have to get it right before the sand of the socially imposed hourglass runs out, lest they risk losing their heads in the cancel culture's guillotine.

One wins the game of Googly Eyes when, despite misperceiving reality, the players get the picture right. Perhaps the artist figures out how to get around the distortions. Perhaps the guesser uses prior efforts to decipher what her teammate is trying to depict. It may be nearly impossible for us to remove our distorting experiences as we struggle to understand, articulate, or answer the challenge of whether Christianity is a white religion. Spending time with one another, learning from one another as teammates, may just give us enough insight to see past the distortions.

Having spent that time with those of diverse backgrounds, I've come to see that when someone claims that Christianity is a white man's religion, the accusation usually is fueled by an amalgam of past facts and present hurts in which Christians have been either complicit or silent. From the transatlantic slave trade to the Jim Crow era to the opposition of women's suffrage, those who bore the moniker Christian participated in and even defended evil actions and discriminatory policies. From the Southern Baptist Convention's prior refusal to admit African Americans to its seminaries to today's headlines of unarmed black men killed by police, white Christians have either campaigned for injustice or have rationalized or downplayed the racial aspects of these incidents. When all of this is lumped together with the fact that nearly 90 percent of Americans who call themselves evangelical are white, it becomes quite easy to see how some confuse aberrant and abhorrent practices with Christianity.[27] Despite being founded by non-whites, despite being populated mostly by non-whites and women, Christianity has come to be seen as the favored religion of white men because Christianity is perceived as the religion manipulated to favor white men.

A black friend's experience with white evangelicalism comes to mind. Lisa Fields is an African American woman who runs a faith-based organization called the Jude 3 Project, the aim of which is to defend the Christian faith while also raising awareness of racial tensions, including within the church. She told my colleagues and me a story that has left its mark. Like all nonprofit organizations, the Jude 3 Project needs funding. Lisa sought advice from the CEO of a major Christian nonprofit on how to get that funding. What she got was hardly encouraging. The CEO told her that she will face three nearly insurmountable challenges: she is black, she is a woman, and she is young. Why were those assets considered liabilities? Youth seen as inexperience is one thing, but her race is at most irrelevant to her mission and at the least an asset. It is this kind of thinking that has perpetuated the perception that Christianity—and by proxy the Christian message—is about and for white men.

That perception, I believe, has come by looking at Christianity through distorted glasses. Likewise, the defenses against that perception also have come by peering through obscured lenses. Facts and emotions blend into a cocktail whose true ingredients are obscured by the unpalatable mixture. The best way to come to achieve clarity is to examine the strongest points of all other perspectives.

This is where we have to deal with some very thorny issues not only as a culture but as a species. The historical and demographical facts show that Christianity has never been solely a white man's religion. In the pages to come, I hope to demonstrate that this truth goes beyond history and demography and is founded upon Scripture and theology. Yet the cultural phenomena, political alliances, self-protective spin, and emotional hurts obscure the very Scripture and theology that can help us heal and move forward. This, however, must not go unsaid: the equality-laced message of the gospel will never be heard if Christian silence about the ugly side of Christendom's history is deafening.

The most obvious and most hideous place to start is the transatlantic slave trade. Describing American support for slavery, African American and Christian author Jemar Tisby writes, "The Civil War paints a vivid picture of what inevitably happens when the American church is complicit in racism and willing to deny the teachings of Jesus to support an immoral, evil institution." Indeed, "people believed in the superiority of the white race and the moral degradation of black people so strongly that they were willing to fight a war over it."[28]

Tisby's words are jarring. One point in his book *The Color of Compromise* is that while the Bible doesn't condone the horrors of slavery, it was used and abused to justify the abomination and further the pursuit of power. Tisby asserts, as I hope to defend within these pages, that the Bible actually speaks *against* the practice of slavery and racism. For now, however, let us come to grips with the fact that Christians were among the slave traders and racists of our past. Tisby's book is an effort to rouse the church to its complicity, or at least its silence, on the evils of racism in America. Until we do so, we will not be able to correct the misperception that Christianity is a white man's religion. I have said this elsewhere, but it is worth repeating here: *the credibility of the message is always judged by the integrity of the messenger.* If the church fails to own up to its checkered past, its integrity will suffer and the credibility of the gospel will be misjudged or, worse, ignored.

This coming to terms with the past creates quite the tension, of course. Some argue that we are dismissing past hurts in our efforts to "move on." Others contend that we will never move on unless we dwell on the positive. Christopher Brooks, a good friend, powerful communicator, and pastor addressed this tension in a way that has had a lasting impact on my thinking. While we were panelists at an event on racial reconciliation and the gospel, someone asked him to comment on whether African Americans dwelling on past wrongs prevents them and white people from working toward continuing progress. As a pastor, Chris has counseled many couples trying to fix their marriages. What he noticed is that the spouse who had been wronged will continually bring up the past incident while the spouse who did the wronging just wants forgiveness, the chance to make things right, and to look to the future. Neither seems to be understanding the motivations of the other—the wronged spouse feeling like the other wants to brush over the deep wounds, while the spouse in the wrong believes the other is intent on perpetually punishing and heaping guilt. Chris pointed out that the one spouse misses the fact that the wounded one needs to process the hurt to move on. The wounded spouse, on the other hand, misses the point that the wrongdoer isn't trying to escape responsibility but is trying to make things right as a means of taking responsibility. Both want to move forward. But forgetting the past trivializes the actions and the pain such that its victim cannot build the future they both want. On the other hand, dwelling on the past prevents healing as well. A balance must be struck if the marriage is to be healed.

We should suck the marrow out of that insight. With open physical wounds, healing takes place only when the skin is brought together by stitches that close the gap. Our cultural skins don't have to look the same for us to heal together. Our racial wounds can start healing when both communities are brought together and try to understand one another's motives. Recognizing the ways in which white people, specifically Christians, have either overtly participated in or complicity allowed racism to happen and persist is an important step. Acknowledging past wrongs affords the wounded in our culture the means by which to process the hurts so that we can forge our future together. This, I believe, is similar to what Jemar Tisby is communicating and is something we would all do well to heed. Otherwise, we will continue to drive forward, changing lanes frequently, heedless of our blind spots.

Historically speaking, Christianity has helped victims to heal their wounds. Black Christians founded the African Methodist Episcopal Church (AME) in the late 1700s because they were removed from white churches or relegated to standing in the back of the church. The founders of the AME didn't see the Christian message as inherently racist. Rather, they saw an inherent dignity preached throughout the Bible that their white brothers and sisters weren't living up to. In other words, as I once heard Dr. Esau

McCaulley put it, the AME Church was started by blacks who thought white people weren't being Christian enough. The AME's founders didn't see anything in Christianity that condoned slavery. In fact, to be a member of the AME Church, one had to affirm an opposition to slavery.

Black Christians in America's early days coupled conservative Bible reading and theology with social critique and the pursuit of justice. Much later, white seminarians and theologians interpreted the Bible more liberally and figuratively because, among other reasons, they were embarrassed by Old Testament passages that seemed to condone slavery. These white theologians felt that Christian social critique and activism would not progress without liberalized interpretations of Scripture. Theologically conservative (and usually white) Christians reacted to the reinterpretation of Scripture by charging progressives with conforming the Bible to fit the times instead of interpreting the times through the lens of the Bible. They suspected that progressive theologians lifted social critique, including about race relations, above biblical primacy. Some conservatives thus withdrew from being outspoken social critics and instead focused on evangelism. Progressives saw this as a kind of fundamentalism that chose the status quo over equal justice. The conservative camp remained largely white and male while the progressive camp's ethnicity grew more diverse as they became more publicly visible. Thus, at least in part, American evangelicalism has come to be seen as a white man's religion.[29]

A false dichotomy has thus formed. Conservative Christians suspect that the "social gospel" redefines the Bible's main message, which is that Jesus came to save the world from sin. Progressives fear that emphasis on biblical conservatism redefines Jesus' message of social change. Both sides fear that the heart of Christianity is being redefined to fit each other's preferences. Yet all the while, many theologically conservative black Christians have maintained a fealty to Scripture and a concern to engage social challenges. Both black and white Christians, women and men, have lived out their faiths to bring dignity and justice in the private lives of unknown people and in national scale movements.

A friend shared an experience he had that explodes the false dichotomy. Before getting into vocational ministry, he worked as a high-level manager for a major company. The human resources department consulted him about some proposed personnel cuts. He learned that a particular employee who might be let go was an African American woman. Wanting to make sure that the decision about her had nothing to do with her race or gender, he met with her, had management meet with her, and reviewed her performance. Eventually some jobs were saved, including hers. My friend hadn't worked with her except for this incident. He went on with his life and she with hers. Years later she reached out to him through social media. She saw his name, saw that he had become a pastor, and was desperate to talk with him. She told him how his care and concern inspired her, how she knew that he was a Christian, and how she somehow coupled his concern for her equal treatment with his faith even though she was not a Christian. Something in the way he comported himself made it obvious that his faith in Christ impelled his behavior. What he did for her played a significant role in her investigating the Christian faith, and she eventually put her faith in Christ—not just as social reformer, but as her Savior. My friend was not her white savior. He merely lived in a way that pointed her to the Savior of the world. My friend didn't need to redefine his biblically conservative ideals to act in a socially responsible way. And the African American woman didn't need to embrace a compromised interpretation of Scripture to see the power in the message that transformed them both.

The gospel message need not be redefined for the sake of justice. Leonard Ravenhill's words come to mind: "The world is not waiting for a new definition of the gospel, but a new demonstration of the gospel's power."[30] We must shed the googly-eyed glasses if we are to see this critical truth.

ACKNOWLEDGING THE PAST, WORKING ON THE PRESENT, AND LOOKING TO THE FUTURE

Acknowledging the failings of our past (and present) doesn't have to mean ignoring our past (and current) triumphs. Failure to recognize those triumphs can lead to a despair that gives way to bitterness. Those triumphs, while only steps along the long road to reconciliation and equality, provide us with hope because they are the evidence that things can and have changed. Let's reconsider Tisby's comment about the American Civil War, for example. "People believed in the superiority of the white race and the moral degradation of black people so strongly that they were willing to fight a war over it." He's right, but isn't the converse also true? Many people believed in the abolition of slavery so strongly that they were willing to fight a war to end it.

The United States' unity was worth risking if it meant slavery could end. The most destructive war in America's history easily could have been avoided through even more compromises than Tisby laments. Compromises easily could have been made, as they had been in the past, if it meant saving the Union. Slavery advocates were using the Bible to justify the institution. For the sake of the Union, Northern Christians could have conceded it was at least arguable that slavery is compatible with the Bible, making it permissible for each state's legislature to decide the matter. Yet they refused to capitulate to an unholy reinterpretation of Scripture because it wasn't arguable that the institution of slavery was biblically justifiable. They wouldn't concede just to preserve a union whose bricks were mortared together with the blood and sweat of slaves. Just as it is sobering to consider Christian complicity in race-based chattel slavery, it is heartening to consider how convicted Christians were that the Bible not only stood against race-based and chattel slavery but also commanded them to risk everything to end the barbarism. To sacrifice one's life—all that one may ever know—to help someone else is to submit oneself to suffering so that others may be liberated from it.

What could be more Christlike? Yes, focusing on the past can be painful, but it can also be inspiring. Indeed, Tisby says as much. "Christianity has an inspiring history of working for racial equity and the dignity of all people, a history that should never be overlooked."[31] Human history isn't so neat and tidy that it must be a picture of either depravity or dignity, either helplessness or hope. It is often a mixture.

History as an academic pursuit is about the piecing together of facts to understand what happened in the past. Social commentary, in its most academic form, simply reports facts, including disparate impacts of policy on diverse groups. Yet history and social commentary are not sterile, video camera–like accounts of what happened or is happening. With our human biases and agendas, we look back and we look forward with googly eyes, sometimes drawing a picture that is not so distorted that we can't piece together what really happened, sometimes drawing something laughably (sometimes tragically) far from reality. Propelled into urgency by the social surge to see Christianity as a tool of Western male oppression, we miss the fact that Christianity was started in the Middle East and flocked to by slaves and women, and then prompted the West to see all people as equally valuable. We miss the fact that most of the Christian world today is neither white nor male. We also look through our googly-eyed glasses and fail to see that decades of institutional racism and pervasive sexism have left their mark on women and non-white communities, and that contemporary strides to end racism and misogyny, as effective as they have been, have not yet gotten us where we should be.

Historical facts and social policies have moral implications, but they are not, in and of themselves, the sources of morality. Rather, they are the expressions of morality. In short, history and policy don't ground the objective morality about the equality of all people. The moral pursuit to end racism and sexism has only one logically legitimate foundation. The conversation I had with the African American man that day over pizza centered on that foundation, and it led to a fruitful discussion filled with understanding instead of angst. Let us consider that conversation and the foundation that was its subject.

CHAPTER 3

THE MORAL HEART OF
THE SOCIAL MATTER

HEARTS AND MINDS MEETING
ON THE UNHURRIED PATH

My pizza-and-cola-fueled conversation with the African American man wasn't under the pressure of a plastic hourglass. We took our time listening and speaking, which is all too rare. He not only wanted to be heard but also to hear. Usually we feign patience in conversations by nodding our heads as the other person is speaking, saying "uh-huh" just enough times to appear interested, all the while bursting inside for our chance to speak. It's a phenomenon I've seen often, one I've come to call "Yeahbut Syndrome." We listen only enough to sense a break in the other person's point long enough for us to interject, "Yeah, but . . . ," and then follow it up with the argument we were going to give regardless of what we just heard. We demand to be understood, and we race past the process of understanding. This young man, however, did exactly the opposite and inspired me to do the same.

He listed some of the typical passages that skeptics lob, which on their face seem to endorse the practices of slavery and ethnic favoritism. I had to fight off my own Yeahbut Syndrome. More than that, I had to concentrate without thinking about how much I was fending off my urge to interrupt so that I could actually hear him. Sincerely listening was not just courteous, it was crucial, because as he spoke, it became clear that his (mis)understandings of those Bible passages weren't the root of the issue; the morality underlying those passages was. Starting there—with the foundations of the morality of human equality—was key. The passages he found troubling didn't cause his outrage at racism and slavery; they fueled it. His sense of objective morality—that racism and slavery are wrong regardless of human opinion—are what drove him to accept the mischaracterizations of those verses. Our conversation would never go from being interesting to being important until we discussed what legitimized his moral outrage.

"You're obviously making these objections from a deep-seated notion of equality and fairness," I said after some time. Indeed, the restrained pathos in his voice conveyed that his heart beat to the rhythm of justice. "Can I ask you something?" I continued. "What rationally justifies the idea of human equality? If we're all just chemical machines or the products of mindless evolution, how is the justice and equality you clearly value any more than a convenient fiction we use to fool ourselves into being nice to each other?" I took a risk asking that question because it could have easily seemed like a dodge, a way to avoid addressing the troubling passages of the Bible. I was grateful the young man didn't see it that way.

In fact, his ready response revealed that he'd already given that quite a bit of thought. "We don't need God to have objective morality. We can observe and measure morality through science." He continued, "Something is morally good if it leads to the flourishing of the greatest number of people or prevents suffering from the greatest number of people. We can scientifically measure what actions lead to flourishing. We know what's morally bad by seeing what unnecessarily harms people."

He was relying heavily on the book *The Moral Landscape*, in which atheist Sam Harris argues that morality is determined by measuring human flourishing and suffering through scientific means.[1] Human flourishing gets us to the moral peaks while suffering and harm put us in the moral valleys, thus the "moral landscape." "Racism," the young man continued, "is objectively immoral because through science we learn that it puts us all in a moral valley. Racism and slavery subject a lot of people to unnecessary suffering, which eventually leads to even more people suffering. We can measure that suffering scientifically. When we see more equality in a society, we can scientifically measure the flourishing. If we have scientific measurements of what's good and bad for people, we can scientifically arrive at objective morality. So why do we need to add God to the analysis?"

The familiar instinct to retort rose up, as if the words were trying to leap from my throat. But it was imperative that I listened, not only to understand his logic but also so that I could understand him as a person. As a young black man with such a fascinating story, he had undoubtedly experienced his unfair share of racism and identity crises. No matter how academic the discussion, no matter how philosophical a turn a conversation takes, morality applies to each of us personally. We have felt the sting of immoral whips and the balm of moral salves. Pain and pleasure have a way of shaping our thinking, of drawing us toward particular conclusions. This is the tension between personally felt and objectively real morality. We feel the effects of good and evil individually and as a community, yet we engage our reason to uncover that which is objectively good or evil. Neither emotion nor reason creates morality. But they are the left and right eyes that allow us to perceive and understand morality. The Christian faith recognizes the bridges between the head and the heart, between logic and experience, between rationality and suffering. That's why, in the midst of an entire people's anguish due to national sin and lawlessness, God bids the Israelites, "Come now, let us reason together" (Isa. 1:18).

Whether regarding racism or sexism, wrestling toward a robust understanding of what makes morality objective doesn't ignore the question of whether the Bible condones these evils. Nor does it ignore the personal pains that such evils cause. In fact, grounding morality in a transcendent source honors those pains by vaulting them beyond the backyard of personal importance and into the realm of objective significance.

SCALING THE MORAL MOUNTAIN

If moral values and duties like treating people equally regardless of race or sex isn't objectively grounded, then moral criticisms of the Bible aren't objectively grounded either. Morality is objective if it doesn't depend on human opinion. If morality does depend on human opinion, then it ceases to be objective. It would be the very definition of subjective.

This, I responded to the African American man, is the chief flaw in Harris's argument for the scientific grounding for objective morality. Harris assumes that human flourishing is morally good. While that may seem self-evident, careful thought shows it to be unwarranted—unless there is a God. Without God, human flourishing is morally no better and morally no worse than the flourishing of viruses or Asian carp. According to Harris, we, like all other animals, are just varyingly complex chemical machines. Humans just happen to be more complex. So the question remains: what is moral about the flourishing of machines? Well, nothing in an objective sense. While flourishing might be *biologically* good for humans, just as it is for cuttlefish, it isn't *morally* good. And human flourishing might not be good for other species. To call it moral is to import an idea completely foreign to atheistic naturalism. Harris argues that we can determine what is objectively morally good by measuring human flourishing because human flourishing is morally good. By assuming, without explanation or justification, that human flourishing is morally good, Harris ends up arguing in a circle.

Indeed, it's difficult to see how Harris could even find himself in that circle in the first place given that he is a determinist. He believes that humans don't actually have free will. Indeed, he believes this so strongly that he wrote an entire book arguing that we have no free will (a book I assume he freely chose to write).[2] We simply act in certain ways based on how our individual biochemical makeups respond to external stimuli. With that kind of picture of humanity, it's difficult (I would venture to say impossible) to conceive of how anything we do is actually moral or immoral. Morality entails choices, after all. Without freely made choices, we cannot be praised or blamed for our decisions and the consequences that follow. I cannot be blamed for blinking when a bug flies at my eyes, for I don't choose to blink. But I can be blamed for turning a blind eye to someone else's suffering if

I had the power and responsibility to do something about it. While we can measure the effects of what we do and don't do, in a mechanistically determined world, none of what we do is by choice. Thus, the effects of our actions are neither moral nor immoral.

This would be true of racism and sexism in a purely naturalistic paradigm. If there is no transcendent moral value giver, then there is no objective moral value. And if there is no objective moral value, then people don't have objective moral value. And if people in general don't have objective moral value, then there remains no objective moral duty for one subset of people to treat another subset with an equal value that neither of them possesses. Treating others like property or as if they are beneath us wouldn't be morally wrong. It would just be—quite literally—a brute reality.

Charles Darwin, one of the fathers of the theory of evolution-driven speciation, worried that his theory could lead to the abolition of morality and the devaluing of other human beings. His entire theory, absent some divine hand behind it, presupposes that some members of a species are better suited to survive and thrive than others. Morality doesn't come into play at all; it's just a matter of "survival of the fittest." This means that by operation of physical law, members of a species with genetically and physically advantageous features consume scarce resources and reproduce more effectively and to the detriment of their genetically and physically disadvantaged competitors. That is, by definition, a paradigm built on inequality, not equality. Any idea of equality between different species and even among members of that same species would be an illusion at best. In Darwin's own words:

> At some future period, not very distant as measured by centuries, the civilized races of man will almost certainly exterminate

and replace throughout the world the savage races. . . . The break will then be rendered wider, for it will intervene between man in a more civilized state, as we may hope, than the Caucasian, and some ape as low as a baboon, instead of as at present between the negro or Australian and the gorilla.[3]

This isn't to say that those who ascribe to naturalistic evolution have come to embrace racism or sexism in some form. It implies, however, that evolution unguided by a divine hand does not justify morality but, on the contrary, has been used to justify prejudices. Historian Richard Weikart has it right when he says that "Darwinism by itself did not produce the Holocaust, but without Darwinism, especially in its social Darwinist and eugenics permutations, neither Hitler nor his Nazi followers would have the necessary scientific underpinning to convince themselves and their collaborators that one of the world's greatest atrocities was really morally praiseworthy."[4]

Philosopher Michael Ruse admits that if there is no God behind human existence, morality is nothing more than an evolutionary ruse (pun intended) that propagates the human species. "Morality is just a matter of emotions, like liking ice cream and sex and hating toothaches and marking student papers," he says. "Now that you know morality is an illusion put in place by your genes to make you a social cooperator, what's to stop you from behaving like an ancient Roman? Well, nothing in an objective sense."[5] Let us not forget that ancient Romans didn't see every human being as an equal or even as a person. Without God as the objective point of reference, there is nothing to stop us from embracing our Roman precursors' view.

If maximized human flourishing is the primary goal or indicator of morality, what then if, based on current circumstances, it would be best to enslave or otherwise oppress some people so that many more could flourish? We need not rely on imagination to see this point. Some of what we enjoy today in the developed world with powerful economies is the fruit of past slaveries or even extant labor oppressions. In the not too distant past, slavery and child labor were so entrenched in society because they were seen as the engine behind human flourishing for the masses. But, one might argue, we should work toward creating a system where we wouldn't need anyone's oppression for maximized flourishing. This doesn't defeat the point, however. One could retort that we should employ such a system until we figure out how to increase flourishing without oppression of a minority populace. Until then, if morality is measured by maximized flourishing, it would be "moral" for us to oppress certain people in the short term if doing so serves the greater good. That would put us on a peak of the moral landscape until we discovered a higher one. Yet each of us recognizes that such a peak is nothing more than a moral valley.

A transcendent view of moral values and duties is what compelled and impelled so many civil rights leaders in America and the anti-apartheid activists of South Africa to work for fundamental change. A cynic could argue that such men and women had nothing more to lose. They were already on the bottom rung of the social and legal ladders. Their struggles to end racial discrimination were merely utilitarian—they didn't have something, so they fought to get it. What could be more evolutionary than the struggle for resources? There's nothing objectively moral about that; rather, they wanted to be at the peak of the landscape with everyone else. I find it particularly fascinating that no one actually voices this argument, no matter how committed to naturalism they are. Perhaps they restrain themselves from reducing the struggle for civil rights to an evolutionary struggle because it would reduce oppressed peoples to the mere animals that their oppressors have thought them to be. Perhaps they don't express this entailment of their view because they know that it cheapens the work of brave men and women who worked for social change. To cheapen those efforts would be, well, immoral. How ironic that some might keep from expressing their amoral beliefs for fear that they might sound immoral. Absent any transcendent basis for morality, however, one would be hard-pressed to show that they are wrong.

But they are wrong, aren't they? A godless account of morality is no account at all. Transcendent, objective moral values only exist if they are grounded in a transcendent moral person. Moral values really make no sense as abstractions. Justice as a mere concept is effete; it does nothing and demands nothing. Love as an abstraction doesn't inspire or impose obligations. A transcendent moral person, whose existence is necessary and independent of human opinion, roots both justice and love, giving them force. A person causes things to happen, can make demands, and can impose obligations. A transcendent moral person grounds the world and our obligations. We owe nothing to love and cannot be beholden to justice. But we owe everything to a personal being who is the very incarnation of love and the determiner of justice. God is that transcendent person who makes moral values like equality real and binding.

Without God, one must ask where our value as people actually comes from. Is our value conferred by other humans? If so, then why do we allow humans the authority to confirm value on a person only to object when a human exercises authority to devalue someone else? Is value confirmed by consensus of culture? If so, how can we say that the power of a culture to confirm such value doesn't also entail the power to take away such value? The answer here is not to ground human equal value in human beings individually or culture at all. History has taught us the folly in that. The answer is to ground human value in the transcendent personhood of God, the uncreated Creator of all things, the ultimate source of all reality, including moral reality.

This has practical implications. A godless view of morality cheapens the efforts of civil rights leaders and those who fought to secure equality for women because it deprives those efforts of their objective moral force. It reduces them to mere competition among animals, some lighter and some darker, some male and some female. Without the transcendent foundation for human equality, it's hard to justify the sacrifices made by those who fought for equality. They sought justice now and also justice enduring. As the billy clubs rained down on a woman's head in South Africa or the noose tightened around a man's neck in the American South, they both realized through slipping consciousness that they were at their earthly end. I wonder if they had the thought, *I'm marching for justice. I will not see that justice in my lifetime because my life has but seconds left. But this was worth it—for the future generation that will see it.* Justice, as a moral category, only exists and only persists past this life if it is grounded in an ultimately just being whose existence transcends our earthly life.

Still, we have to contend with the reality of those who did have much to lose in terms of advantage and privilege in the fights to end racial injustice. I think of F. W. de Klerk, John Wesley, and William Wilberforce to name a few. Pastor James Reeb, a white man, marched with Dr. Martin Luther King Jr. from Selma to Montgomery and died from being badly beaten during the march. Surely Pastor Reeb enjoyed safety, privilege, and maybe even some measure of power. Why give it up for someone else's sake? While none of these men were the white saviors of black men and women, the point remains that their sacrifices to end discrimination in the 1960s were not utilitarian. They were self-sacrificial, just as were the efforts of many more black lives.

Such altruism is sometimes explained away in evolutionary terms. A beaver may risk its life to warn other beavers of a coming predator, for example. This isn't moral, of course. It's merely instinctual. So, too, one might argue, civil rights demonstrators gave up their safety and their lives out of instinct bred into them by evolution, not by some higher moral authority or sense of transcendence. How grotesquely ironic such an analysis would be. At the core of racism is the idea that those of another race are subhuman. Arguing that civil rights activists were acting out of animal instinct plays right into that idea. To retort that evolutionary altruism applies to all races doesn't really rescue the argument because it still reduces the heroism of the past to biology. Hawks are not racist toward field mice. A lion is not racist when it kills another lion with a darker mane. The beaver doesn't have a choice. It doesn't contemplate its own existence, calculate the costs and benefits, and then summon its courage to aid its fellow beavers. But human beings are capable of such things, capable of such courage, having been endowed with those faculties by their Creator. Reducing all of us to animality guts the very idea of justice and cheapens the efforts to end racism and oppression of women. Something more must be going on. That something more is the recognition that moral actions echo beyond our lives, even beyond all earthly lives.

Transcendence is what gives our moral actions objective meaning. On this side of eternity, those who gave their lives to end chattel slavery or during the marches for civil rights may not have seen the progress we've made since then. Those women who went to jail seeking voting rights may not have seen the victories to come. They may not have seen the mountain of work there is yet to do. The reality of existence beyond this life offers the hopeful anticipation that equal treatment and justice will eventually come.

What is justice if there is nothing beyond this life after all? Does it have any real meaning? If this life is all there is and oblivion awaits, then Martin Luther King Jr. and Adolf Hitler have the same destiny. In fact, Hitler would have been better off because he chose his path through suicide and was hoping that there was nothing on the other side. Everyone King has helped will eventually dissolve into oblivion. Everyone Hitler murdered or ruined will come to that same end.

This is worth marinating in for a bit longer. These two men, King and Hitler, couldn't have been more different or had more opposing agendas. Indeed, the lives of these two men give us exactly the kind of comparison we need to see the absurdity of the pursuit of equality and justice absent the existence of a transcendent personal being. King was an African American. He saw himself as the reluctant leader of a campaign of nonviolent resistance against racial inequality. Hitler was an Austrian-born German with ambition to rule the world as Führer of the master race. Famously, King expressed his hope to live in a society one day where all people were judged by the content of their character, not by the color of their skin. Accepting the Nobel Prize for Peace, Dr. King eloquently espoused his belief that "unarmed truth and unconditional love will have the final word in reality."[6] Hitler espoused exactly the opposite. He would have viewed King's aspiration as one coming from a subhuman striving to subdue the aspirations of the *Übermensch*. Flying squarely in the face of King's hope in "unarmed truth and unconditional love," Hitler "freed Germany from the stupid and degrading fallacies of conscience, morality. We will train young people before whom the whole world will tremble. I want young people capable of violence, imperious, relentless, cruel."[7]

Both men died well before either of them would have wanted. King's life was taken by a racist who couldn't stand to see the equality King championed. Hitler's life also was ended by a racist. But he was that racist, preferring suicide over seeing his vision of racial supremacy fail. If there is no God, then oblivion has robbed King of his future hope and has rewarded Hitler with an escape from ultimate justice.

The objective reality of transcendent justice undergirded King's efforts and message. He was too familiar with racist manipulations of the Bible to risk the civil rights movement on a superficial form of Christianity. Indeed, I'm convinced that King, despite his theological idiosyncrasies, understood that absent God's transcendent moral authority, there really is no obligation for groups of people to champion the betterment of others. "I refuse to accept the idea that the 'isles' of man's present nature makes him morally incapable of reaching up for the eternal 'oughtness' that forever confronts him," he wrote.[8] By referencing the "eternal oughtness," King avoided the "is/ought" fallacy of moral philosophy, which is the mistaken assumption that just because certain circumstances exist, it follows that those circumstances ought to change or stay the same. Circumstances only "ought" to be a certain way if there is a transcendent, objective moral standard by which to judge those circumstances and impose an obligation to change or maintain them. Human beings, King noted, fail that standard all the time and therefore cannot be the measuring stick of morality. "Lamentably," he wrote, "it is an historical fact that privileged groups seldom give up their privileges voluntarily. Individuals may see the moral light and voluntarily give up their unjust posture; but, as Reinhold Niebuhr has reminded us, groups tend to be more immoral than individuals."[9] Perhaps this is because we too easily substitute our group's authority for God's. King was far too savvy to think that fleeting sentimentality could withstand that tendency. Instead, he masterfully addressed the transcendent foundation upon which the philosophical scaffolding of equality is built.

We would do well to heed the wisdom of Carl Ellis Jr., an African American scholar who understands that scrubbing God from the moral imperative of ending racism would be fatal to that very endeavor. "White historians sold us a bill of goods by leaving Black folks out," he writes. "Black secularists sold us a bill of goods by leaving God out."[10] This holds true whether we are addressing racism or sexism.

SIMPLE BUT NOT SIMPLISTIC

A particular danger in advocating that spiritual truths can cure social ills is to succumb to simplistic solutions. We must carefully distinguish between simplistic solutions—which usually don't work—and simple solutions, which may be just what we need. Conceptually, walking across a tightrope is relatively straightforward and simple: maintain balance while placing one foot in front of the other and repeat. Of course, I imagine that anyone who has actually walked a tightrope, especially at a great height, would say that while the concept is simple, the execution is not simplistic.

So, too, with the Christian message of equality regardless of ethnicity or gender. The claim is simple: all human beings are equally made in the image of God (Gen. 1:26–27), which means that ethnic or sex-based inequality is not only factually unfounded but also morally reprehensible. If we all just believed that and lived out that belief, inequality would cease. While the concept is simple, the execution is anything but. Many have tried to walk that tightrope only to lose balance and plunge because they have approached a simple solution simplistically. God anchors the tightrope to the starting point, and the Christian gospel anchors the rope to the ending point. It is simple-sounding enough, but like walking the tightrope, dedication, learning, self-reflection, and courage are crucial to the goal.

Consider the young African American man's chief objections, for example. He fled from Scripture because he read passages that seemed to justify chattel slavery. He believed that the Bible championed ethnic superiority. His objections cannot simply be addressed by showing that absent God, the morality upon which to base our objections to racism doesn't exist. His issue specifically was that the God of the Bible favors certain ethnicities over others and condones human enslavement. Merely quoting the Bible's declaration that all humans bear God's image and that Jesus sacrificed himself because "God so loved the world" is a good starting point, but much more needs to be said, explained, believed, and ultimately lived before those truths will appeal to the wounded heart and concerned mind.

The claim that people just need to hear, understand, and believe the gospel to have their hearts turned away from racism and sexism is a simplistic solution that has been chided as "the miracle motif." The criticism has some weight behind it. Myopic reliance on converting people to have a correct theology has resulted in malaise or apathy about the need for social action.[11] As a follower of Christ, I would love nothing more than for this to be the antidote to the prejudices that poison society. That, unfortunately, isn't the world in which we now or have ever lived.

Yet I hasten to add that something valuable remains in looking to the gospel as a starting point to address how we might end hatred and oppression. The miracle motif, for all its shortcomings, presents the ideal of Christian belief and practice. That is, it presents ideals—objectively rooted ideas not swayed by cultural fashion—to which each of us should aspire. Those ideals flow from the gospel message. The problem, of course, is that almost no one—Christian or otherwise—fully embraces everything their worldview espouses or acts consistently with their worldview's teaching. This is not an indictment of the Christian message but rather a point of credibility in its favor. The Christian message is not and has never been that once a person submits their life to Christ, they instantly will become morally perfect and free from blind spots. On the contrary, the Bible specifically says that once a person begins to follow Christ, the lifelong process of sanctification begins. Sanctification, which basically means "to become holy," is a process that never ends this side of heaven.

We see this process at work in the lives of Jesus' apostles, from Peter to Paul. Peter ascended moral peaks of human equality when he was fueled by the spiritual revelation that the gospel message was offered not only to Jews but also to Gentiles (Acts 10:9–11:18). Yet he descended to the moral valleys when he disregarded fellowship with Gentiles when he was around other Jews (Gal. 2:11–13; Acts 15:1–35). Paul commented that he was given some kind of an affliction (we don't know what it was exactly) that God would not remove from him, to keep him from becoming conceited (2 Cor. 12:7–10). Evidently, pride was something with which Paul, because he was human, wrestled even after his remarkable conversion. It was the same Paul who wrote that even after salvation, he struggled to refrain from doing the things he did not want to do while struggling to do that which he knew he should do (Rom. 7:13–25). Perhaps putting it most plainly, the apostle John told Christians, "If we say we have no sin, we deceive ourselves, and the truth is not in us" (1 John 1:8).

History has borne this out, has it not? Otherwise great men and women in church history have had serious blind spots to their own prejudices. Jonathan Edwards, for example, was a theological giant, and yet for all his insights, he still owned slaves. George Whitefield, another looming figure in Protestantism, preached approximately eighteen thousand times to an estimated 10 million people, including blacks and black slaves. While criticizing the cruel treatment of slaves, Whitefield never seemed to oppose slavery. Some have argued that Whitefield actually supported it. Samuel Sewall, a Puritan minister, presided as one of the judges of the Salem witch trials, which many consider to have been a sort of sexist inquisition. Given these men's obvious grasp of and allegiance to the Bible, one would be hard-pressed to argue that belief in and understanding of the gospel is sufficient to turn a person away from racism or sexism.

The gospel is not like spiritual Nescafé, instantly turning receptive hearers into consistent doers. It is a process, one with fits and starts, but it is valuable nonetheless. Sewall's story is particularly appropriate here because he eventually turned from his grievous errors. He was the only judge to apologize for his role in the Salem witch trials. The entire ordeal may have opened his eyes to the ethnic and gender inequities surrounding him. He wrote one of the earliest American antislavery tracts and one of the first tracts arguing for women's equality.

I also think of how Abraham Lincoln, the Great Emancipator, grew in his thinking on slaves and equality. While he once advocated sending freed slaves to their own colony outside the United

States, toward the end of his life he shifted, looking to meet the challenge of integrating liberated slaves into American society. As Jörg Nagler writes, "[Lincoln] more and more revised his stance after many positive encounters with black troops and many African Americans. There was no more talk of colonization."[12] In his second inaugural speech, Lincoln alluded to the Bible to highlight the horrors of slavery and the God-ordained righteousness it would take to end it. Frederick Douglass, the freed slave who saw the previous contradictions in Lincoln's thinking, was at the inaugural ball following that second address. Lincoln asked Douglass for his opinion of the speech, remarking, "There is no man in the country whose opinion I value more than yours." Douglass responded, "Mr. Lincoln, that was a sacred effort."[13] Perhaps Lincoln's thinking was being sanctified in some way.

Alas, it simply isn't true that common belief automatically leads to the pursuit of the common good. That would not only be a simplistic solution but also a false one. Yet I hasten to add this: only the Christian message offers the necessary condition for overcoming such sinful prejudices in a comprehensive way. Once that condition is met, the subsequent conditions of consistent living, compassion, and self-sacrifice may follow, even with some inconsistency. That is a simple claim, but it is far from simplistic.

A MOTIF WITHOUT A MIRACLE

Paradoxically, something similar to the miracle motif has influenced secular efforts to end racial injustice and sexism through the magic of commonality. How often have we seen sentiments like "There's more that unites us than divides us" adorn car bumpers yet fail to compel change? A debate I attended between secular humanist Christopher DiCarlo and Christian Andy Bannister springs to mind. At the Canadian Museum for Human Rights, they debated the question: "Human Rights: By Design or by Default?"[14] Among other things, Dr. DiCarlo argued that God does not bestow humans with rights. Rather, we have rights by virtue of our existence. Further, he argued, we should protect one another's basic human rights because "We're all African." As he explained it, our evolution from a common ancestor originating in Africa makes us all African and, thus, equal. When we mistreat others, he might argue, we mistreat ourselves.

The debate moderator asked Dr. DiCarlo how his position avoids the "Is/Ought Fallacy," which is the mistaken belief that a moral "ought" (we *should* treat each other equally) logically follows from a factual "is" (we all have a common ancestor). The mere supposed fact of common descent doesn't impose on anyone a moral obligation to act fairly. For instance, the National Basketball Association *is* filled with exceptionally tall people. Yet not every exceptionally tall person *ought* to have a career making millions in professional basketball. While Dr. DiCarlo acknowledged that this fallacy was a hurdle to his view, he ran around the hurdle instead of leaping over it by simplistically responding that we as a species "need to grow up."

This is nothing more than the simplistic miracle motif devoid of the miraculous. In a secularized worldview, we magically conjure up an objective moral obligation to treat each other equally by virtue of our common genetic ancestry. At least the miracle motif as applied to Christianity includes the notion that our common value derives from being valued as children of God, the transcendent moral lawgiver. With his inimitable wit, atheist philosopher

Michael Ruse reveals just how much faith it takes to believe that secular ideas can really get us to believe in universal human equality: "God is dead. Morality has no foundation. Long live morality. Thank goodness!"[15] This is less than a vapid miracle motif. It is nothing more than wistful and magical thinking.

Some have attempted more nuanced secular solutions to the problem of prejudice. I think of the analysis and solutions offered by Ibram X. Kendi in his bestselling book, *How to Be an Antiracist*, a book I practically devoured. Kendi's book startles and provokes thought. Yet for all the praise it received, it left me empty, lacking a proper solution for the problem analyzed. Kendi's baseline is that it is not enough to say something like "I'm not racist" because such an attitude allows a person to remain blind to their covert racism, allows them to hide it from others, prevents them from acting to end racism, or all of the above. Kendi's analysis showers over a broad range of social areas, including race, gender, religion, geography, sexual orientation, and transgenderism. The philosophy of intersectionality flows through his entire book, yet what fascinated me even more was the humanistic undercurrent. Kendi defines a racist as "one who is supporting a racist policy through their actions or inaction or expressing a racist idea."[16] This seemingly straightforward definition cries out to be scrutinized. Kendi goes out of his way not to define a person as a racist, for example, as "someone who views people of other races as inferior to themselves and acts accordingly." In other words, human inclinations toward hatred *aren't* the root of racism. Instead, he writes, "Antiracist ideas argue that racist *policies* are the cause of racial inequities."[17] Kendi claims, "'Racist' and 'antiracist' are like peelable name tags that are placed and replaced based on what someone is doing or not doing, supporting or expressing in each moment."[18] He describes *policies, ideas,* and *actions* as racist, but not the people who implement those policies, hold those ideas, or perform those actions. This theme runs through his entire analysis, culminating ultimately in his proposed solution to racism, which is that we don't need to change people's hearts and minds first. We need to change policy first—and hearts and minds will follow.

This solution follows directly from his view of humanity, which appears to be a mix of humanism (that human beings are essentially good) and existentialism (that our existence precedes our essence and that we are defined by what we do, not by what we are). With rhetorical force, Kendi asks, "What if economic, political, or cultural self-interest drives racist policymakers, not hateful immorality, not ignorance?"[19] He tries to prove that policies change minds (not the other way around) by citing law after law that seems to have changed people's minds after they were enacted. Ultimately, Kendi argues that racism isn't really a product of hateful immorality or ignorance, but of self-interest. In other words, the inherent condition of humanity isn't the underlying problem; the policies we've implemented are the problem.

And yet Kendi decries the idea of first trying to appeal to the consciences of white people or educating them about the plight of people of color because, according to him, such appeals just don't work. Indeed, he claims that mental and educational persuasion—as a prerequisite to policy change—is doomed to failure because policy change will always be accompanied by fear and apathy given that racist policies are adopted to safeguard and protect those with power.[20] Poetically, the title of his chapter on the appeal to the consciences of white people is "Failure." Policy must change *first* because changed policies change people's minds, not the other way around, he argues. Yet there is an inherent tension (if not outright contradiction) in Kendi's analysis and solution. He holds to the humanist belief in the essential moral goodness of people. But he also acknowledges the human tendency to preserve power, even if it means being apathetic to others' suffering. How can he argue that racist policies are *not* driven by hateful immorality and ignorance while simultaneously arguing that they are preserved by apathy and fear? I fail to see the difference. Preserving one's unfair power over others out of apathy and fear sounds very much like hateful immorality to me.

Perhaps Kendi is wrestling with the tension between human dignity and human ignobility. He wants to avoid saying that humans suffer from a sinful condition, yet he recounts numerous experiences in which he, his family, and friends have been victims of human sinfulness. These twin mysterious realities, of human dignity and depravity, are addressed in the Bible—ironically the very source that our culture says is out of touch with today's issues. Within its pages, the Bible describes human beings as "fearfully and wonderfully made" and bearing the very image of God (Ps. 139:14; Gen. 1:26–27). Yet it also tells us that we are beset with conditions of selfishness and evil (Matt. 15:19; Jer. 17:9). Jesus' words about the human condition are more vivid yet. "For out of the heart come evil thoughts, murder, adultery, sexual immorality, theft, false witness, slander" (Matt. 15:19). What we want to hear, and what Kendi wants to believe, is that human beings can appeal to the better angels of our nature to overcome the policies that hold others down. But Jesus tells us what we need to hear, which is that evil policies don't arise in a vacuum. They sprout from the evil that wells up in the human heart. I dare say Kendi may recognize this, at least implicitly. As he concludes the opening chapter of his book, he writes, "To be an antiracist is a radical choice in the face of this history [of racist policies], requiring a radical reorientation of our consciousness."[21] I agree entirely with that sentence. But I am puzzled as to how he moves from that statement at the beginning of the book to an entire chapter near the end arguing that any effort to reorient our conscience is doomed to failure. Perhaps the problem lies not with Kendi, but with the incoherence of secular humanistic beliefs and the idea that we can radically reorient our thinking by sheer force of human will. For Jesus, the human will itself is the problem.

Experiencing the hell of being jailed and tortured for his efforts to end racism led John Perkins to understand our need for God. "I saw something that cannot be humanly overcome. Only the love of God could overcome such evil. I knew that if I didn't forgive, I would be overcome by the same darkness. I purposed at that moment to preach the gospel strong enough to win whites and blacks—to burn through the bigotry and hatred of racism."[22] Perkins saw that only a reliance on the intrinsic value of *all* human beings—a value founded in God as our Creator—could end the scourge. "In God's economy," Perkins continues, "each individual was to be enriched by the other: our people were to benefit from the bounty of the white who had become enriched by free labor; the whites were to benefit from the character building truths that blacks had learned throughout and because of slavery."[23]

The Bible, with its accurate depiction of human complexity, acknowledges and resolves the tension we saw in Kendi's analysis. This is not to say that Kendi and secular thinkers are entirely wrong in believing that policy change can effectuate individual or societal change. I agree with Kendi that people are influenced by policies. But I disagree with his assertion that policy change is the primary or only way forward. Policy and heart changes can happen simultaneously, so long as changes of the heart remain the necessary condition for societal change. Contrary to what Kendi argues, policies won't change until the hearts and minds of those who make the policies change. Yes, more African Americans in positions of influence can change the legislative bodies that make our laws and the executive branches that enforce them. But there will also need to be changes of hearts and minds, lest resentment build and, like Pharaoh in Moses' day, those enslaved by avarice and self-interest try to resist the social and political changes. Indeed, Kendi admits as much. The point I wish to make here is that addressing the sinfulness of the human heart through the transcendent source that can change it *coupled with* the implementation and enforcement of equitable policies are the two constants that make the equality equation solvable.

Robin DiAngelo's wildly popular book, *White Fragility: Why It's So Hard for White People to Talk about Racism*, offers another fascinating look at secular efforts to address racism.[24] Dr. DiAngelo's basic premise is that white people get very defensive when confronted with the possibility that they have been either overtly or inadvertently racist. To address their racism, white people ought to engage in perpetual introspection and should be open to learning about their witting or unwitting participation in racialization and racism. DiAngelo does us a service insofar as she describes ways in which our reactions to racism might shut down important conversations and even further perpetuate racism. But in much of what she writes, one can't help but sense the inherent contradictions that plague her efforts. Somewhat contrary to Kendi, DiAngelo argues that not just policies or structures are racist, but people are racist too. While structures might perpetuate racism, racist people created those structures. Yet while emphasizing the problem with racist people, DiAngelo asserts that racism isn't really a moral issue. "Being good or bad," she states plainly, "is not relevant."[25] Rather, racism is a product of socialization based on culture and background that leads to sometimes conscious, but usually unconscious biases against those of a different race—predominantly black people in the West. It's fascinating that DiAngelo tries so hard to decouple racism from morality, all the while believing that we *ought* (a moral term) to confront and change our unconscious biases. Again, we are left with a secular effort at addressing racism devoid of any basis on which to confront its evils. It would take a miracle for such a solution to actually solve anything.

DiAngelo provides at least one valuable insight, and we would do well to shine a light on it. Her insight regarding unconscious racism comports with the Christian teaching that our ability to know right and wrong has been impaired since the moral fall of Adam and Eve. In Christian terms, this impairment is called the noetic effect of sin—the condition of sin prevents us from seeing things clearly. Where DiAngelo parts ways with the Christian concept (and where I humbly assert that she goes wrong) is when she equates *unconscious* with *amoral*. For her, to the extent that racism is unconscious, it cannot be immoral because morality entails a conscious choice. But an immorality that is unconscious is no less immoral. In fact, oftentimes such morality is not as much unconscious as it is *subconscious*. We know that sin lurks in our souls (DiAngelo, for example, knows her racial biases exist), but we suppress that knowledge—to hide it from our conscious awareness—to make ourselves feel better. Is that not a moral choice? DiAngelo pays lip service to an aspect of the human condition to which the Bible gives full voice. Indeed, at one point, DiAngelo seems to recognize that the human condition is the real underlying problem. "My psychosocial development was inculcated in a white supremacist culture in which I am the superior group," she writes. "Telling me to treat everyone the same is not enough to override this socialization; nor is it humanly possible."[26]

What a fascinating statement. She is correct in acknowledging this isn't possible looking humanward. But perhaps we ought to consider what is possible if we start by looking Godward.

This is what the gospel—the good news—is all about. We get the privilege of participation in the resultant change. It is God who saves and God who transforms, but we are active participants in the process. You must "work out your own salvation with fear and trembling," the apostle Paul wrote (Phil. 2:12). Applied to racism and sexism, the good news is that we do not solely rely on correct beliefs; we utilize those beliefs to fuel action.

Even when laws change, society is still in need of change. Slavery has been abolished for a century and a half in the United States, and sweeping civil rights legislation was implemented in the late 1960s, outlawing racial discrimination and segregation. Yet racism persists fifty years later. Relying *merely* on legal reform to change culture is just as much a miracle motif as relying on common ancestry or common religion. Paul and Jesus sought more. They sought mind and heart transformation.

The person of Christ and his message radically transformed my friend Tom Tarrants. He grew up in a Christian home, but the message didn't take root in his heart. Nourished by the false ideologies of the Ku Klux Klan and others, Tom's hatred for Jews and blacks grew. Eventually he saw the United States government as complicit in helping to advance a Marxism that would deprive whites of power and give it to blacks and Jews. He baptized his hatred with skewed interpretations of the Bible, which drove him to participate in a scheme to bomb a government building. He went to prison after the scheme was foiled. There, a desire to know the truth, regardless of his preferences, began to take root. Ultimately, he saw in the pages of Scripture a description of his own sin and the value of others regardless of race. Encountering African Americans went a long way to putting those truths into practice. He went from an angry, ignorant, hate-filled terrorist to an activist for racial reconciliation. To know Tom now and to hear his past history is to flirt with dysphoria. How can it be that this slow-talking, gentle man was once shot multiple times in an attempted bombing of a government building as a Ku Klux Klan member? Changed policies didn't change Tom Tarrants's heart or his actions. It was Christ and his example to love those different from us that inclined Tom's heart toward equality and reconciliation.[27]

A fully orbed understanding of how transcendent truths intersect our earthbound problems diverts us around the rocks of the is/ought fallacy. The Christian faith supplies the necessary condition of "eternal oughtness" that grounds the policies we need to address the problematic "is" in our culture. Such an understanding also invigorates an otherwise anemic miracle motif with the motivation for action. C. S. Lewis was insightful here. "Theology teaches what ends are desirable and what means are lawful," he wrote, "while Politics teaches what means are effective. Thus Theology tells us that every man ought to have a decent wage. Politics tells by what means this is likely to be attained. Theology tells us which of these means are consistent with justice and charity. On the political question, guidance comes not from Revelation but from natural prudence, knowledge of complicated facts and ripe experience."[28]

A poem by John Greenleaf Whittier titled "The Cross" couples the gospel message with actions that effectuate equality and justice. Whittier penned this poem about Richard Dillingham, who died in prison for trying to help runaway slaves escape.

> "The cross, if rightly borne, shall be
> No burden, but support to thee;"
> So, moved of old time for our sake,
> The holy monk of Kempen spake.
>
> Thou brave and true one! Upon whom
> Was laid the cross of martyrdom,
> How didst thou, in thy generous youth,
> Bear witness to this blessed truth!
>
> Thy cross of suffering and of shame
> A staff within thy hands became,
> In paths where faith alone could see
> The Master's steps supporting thee.
>
> Thine was the seed-time; God alone
> Beholds the end of what is sown;
> Beyond our vision, weak and dim,
> The harvest-time is hid with Him.
>
> Yet, unforgettable where it lies,
> That seed of generous sacrifice,
> Though seeming on the desert cast,
> Shall rise with bloom and fruit at last.[29]

Humanity is much messier than either of these simple solutions. The Bible has recognized this for centuries. The question for us now is whether the Bible really teaches ethnic and gender equality. It has been challenged on these fronts for some time now, so it is time for us to address this challenge.

NOT JUST FOR WHITES ONLY

PART 1

NOT JUST FOR
WHITES ONLY

CHAPTER 4

SCRIPTURE, SLAVERY, AND RACE

SLAVERY AND THE BIBLE

The African American man with whom I pondered over pizza was willing to consider that his objections to the Bible had no basis unless morality is rooted in God. But, he pointed out, his problems with the Bible's passages about slavery couldn't be fixed just by pointing to God as the source of objective morality. He was right, of course. If the Bible condones evils such as racism and slavery, then the God it describes as its author cannot be the grounding for moral good; we'd have to search elsewhere for that God. What was left for us to wrestle with was whether the God of the Bible actually condones those evils.

It isn't difficult to see how this man could conclude that the Bible does condone such evils as racism and slavery. The Old Testament laws seem to allow for the ownership, acquisition, selling, and treatment of *'ebed*, a word that is often translated from Hebrew into English as *slave*. Similarly, the New Testament makes references to *doulos*, a Greek word sometimes translated into English as "slave." The potency here is not just that the Bible uses these words, but that it uses *'ebed* and *doulos* in passages that seem to regulate and even condone slavery. The question the young man and I wrestled with— the question with which we wrestle here—is whether the Bible condones and regulates the acquisition of human beings for involuntary labor like the slavery practiced in the antebellum American South and other parts of the world. Those institutionalized trades trafficked in human beings by forcibly ripping them from homes to be sold as subhuman property with no hope of future liberty.

"That's exactly what the Bible allows," the young man pressed. "It has specific laws allowing for and regulating the ownership of human beings as slave labor. So at least in the Old Testament Law, God institutionalized slavery." He listed a few passages from the Bible, merely as examples of the many, where this seems to be the case. Exodus 21:1–32 lists various laws about the treatment of "slaves." It reads, "When you buy a Hebrew slave . . ." and "When a man sells his daughter as a slave," for example (Ex. 21:2, 7). In particular, he referenced these two passages from the law of Moses to make his point:

> "As for your male and female slaves whom you may have: you may buy male and female slaves from among the nations that are around you. You may also buy from among the strangers who sojourn with you and their clans that are with you, who have been born in your land, and they may be your property." (Lev. 25:44–45)

> "When a man strikes his slave, male or female, with a rod and the slave dies under his hand, he shall be avenged. But if the

slave survives a day or two, he is not be avenged, for the slave is his money." (Ex. 21:20–21)

"Why should I believe in a God like that?" he asked.

"The New Testament really isn't any better," he continued. Nowhere in the New Testament do we see a condemnation of slavery. In fact, he said, the New Testament tells slaves to remain that way and be content with their spiritual freedom. He was referring to Ephesians 6:5–6, where Paul wrote, "Slaves, be obedient to those who are your masters according to the flesh, with fear and trembling, in the sincerity of your heart, as to Christ; not by way of eye-service, as people-pleasers, but as slaves of Christ, doing the will of God from the heart" (NASB). Though he didn't bring it up, others have claimed that the apostle Peter paired submission to slavery with faithfulness to Christ when he wrote, "Submit yourselves for the Lord's sake to every human authority. . . . Slaves, in reverent fear of God submit yourselves to your masters, not only to those who are good and considerate, but also to those who are harsh" (1 Peter 2:13, 18 NIV). This brings to mind reflections by former slave Nancy Ambrose. She told her grandson, Howard Thurman, how painful it was to hear Paul's words used by her master's minister. "During the days of slavery . . . the master's minister would occasionally hold services for the slaves," she described. "At least four or five times a year he used as a text: 'Slaves, be obedient to them that are your masters.' I promised my Maker that if I ever learned to read and if freedom ever came, I would not read that part of the Bible."[1] The depth of that tragedy cannot be gainsaid.

These were among the biblical passages that slave traders, slave owners, and those otherwise in favor of the practice used to try to justify it. Again, the African American man asked me, "If there is a God, why would I believe in a God like this?"

Whether we see a distant image accurately depends on the lens through which we view it. The simplest telescopes have two lenses. One holds the smaller lens closest to one's eye. The larger lens is at the end of the telescope's barrel. When they work together, they magnify the faraway image to give a clearer view of what it's really like. If the smaller, closer lens is tinted, it alters the accuracy of the image. I feel that something similar has happened with our view of the Bible.

In our closer history, the transatlantic slave trade was institutionalized, based on forced labor, and was largely race-based. The tint of that nearer history explains, at least in large part, why we equate the Bible's regulations and descriptions of servitude with the race-based horrors of our not-too-distant past. The young man I was conversing with was peering through a tinted lens. Like many of us, he had difficulty seeing that none of the Bible's regulations on servitude call for the involuntary enslavement of people because of their ethnicity. Past efforts of proslavery advocates to baptize racial enslavement through the twisting of Scripture have only tinted our lenses further. The reality, however, remains unaltered.

Gregory of Nyssa, one of the Cappadocian fathers, is considered the first person in history not just to decry the treatment of slaves but to reject slavery altogether.[2] The Bible laid the groundwork for his activism. And while abolitionist Christians had been directly challenging the institution of slavery since as far back as the fourth century AD—fourteen hundred years before slavery ended in America—slavery advocates who also called themselves Christians countered with the verses the young man listed, among others. That countermove was dishonest, however, because those verses had to be manipulated, torn from their broader contexts and skewed, to justify race-based chattel slavery. The proslavery crowd knew it too. They knew that the Bible, properly interpreted and lived out, preached liberty and human dignity. That's why, as scholars like Carl Ellis Jr. have noted, there was an initial resistance to evangelizing African slaves. Slaveowners and traders feared that the slaves would recognize the Bible's stand against oppression and its stand for liberty, embrace that message, and use it to petition for their own freedom. Those enslavers turned out to be right. Just as water will steadily split a boulder or penetrate granite, so the gospel penetrated the mortar of the slavers' walls and wound its way into the hearts and minds of African descended slaves, pointing them to a hope of multifaceted freedom.

In this, I am reminded of the film *Amistad*, which is based on the true story of Africans illegally seized from their homes and sold into slavery.[3] During their voyage to the Americas, the slaves revolt and take over the slave ship *La Amistad*. Through various storms (literal and figurative ones), the ship eventually arrives in the American North. A complicated court case ensues over whether the Africans are merely property that should be returned to their captors or executed for mutiny. A particularly powerful scene depicts the slaves in a crowded holding cell, awaiting their fate. One of the slaves, a man named Cinqué, has come to be in possession of a Bible. He doesn't understand English but gets the story of Jesus' life from the pictures in that Bible. A fellow prisoner asks him about what he's looking at. Cinqué goes through the images with him, explaining the story they tell.

Cinqué identifies with the suffering of Jesus' people. He recognizes that Jesus changed everything; he healed people and protected them. As he progresses through the pictures, Cinqué shows his fellow prisoner images of Jesus being bound and put on trial. "He must have done something," his fellow prisoner says. But seeing that the character of Christ didn't fit with his being a criminal, Cinqué responds, "Why? What did *we* do?" Cinqué identifies with Jesus in a profound way while in prison for doing nothing more than standing up for his own dignity. As he examines images of Jesus' death and resurrection, he sees the possibility of hope and freedom, in of all places, a prison full of slaves.

Another powerful scene depicts the judge's delivery of the verdict on the Africans' fate. As the court reads its verdict that they are in fact not property and that their rebellion on board the ship was justified, a mixture of outrage and jubilation erupts. As the Africans celebrate, Cinqué holds up his Bible with both hands, recognizing that the hope promised in the gospel can be filled both in this life and the life to come. Not even a language barrier was enough to stem the tide of gospel hope.

Cinqué had only images to go on—he could not read the Bible and thus couldn't have known about the passages that troubled the young African American man with whom I was conversing. But other slaves knew about those passages and yet plunged into the Christian message anyway. Once that happened, their masters and traffickers needed to hold back the flood. They filled their sandbags with manipulations of Paul's and Peter's words in efforts to convince Christian slaves that it was their Christian duty to be content with their enslavement. The sandbags were not enough. Many slaves drank in the freedom the gospel championed.

SERVITUDE, NOT SLAVERY

What makes biblically regulated slavery different from modern-day slavery is that the Bible didn't really regulate slavery per se. That is to say, what the Bible regulated was not involuntary chattel slavery but voluntary and temporary servitude. There is a perceived difference between Hebrew slaves and foreign slaves, which we will address. This, of course leads to the question of why the Bible (including the passages I referenced above) mentions "slaves" within the context of biblical law. The answer is that the Hebrew word *'ebed* is capable of being translated different ways. "The Hebrew term for servant or slave (*'ebed*) is a neutral word that denotes a dependency relationship rather than degradation, property ownership, or oppression. It often can function as an honorific title. For example, after their deaths both Moses and Joshua are called 'the servant [*'ebed*] of the LORD.'"[4] My name in Arabic is derived from the same Semitic roots as Hebrew. The many millions around the world who share that name or something similar know that it doesn't convey something degrading. Rather, it acknowledges a faithful dependence on and service to God. *'Ebed* can mean "slave," as in a person who is owned as property, depending on the context. Likewise, it can also describe a voluntary servant or even a royal official (see, for example, 1 Kings 9:22 and 2 Kings 25:24). Because we have come to think of the word *slave* as univocally meaning a person treated as property and forced into someone else's service, we miss the important shades of meaning in how the Bible uses the word *'ebed*.

To convey the less odious shades intended by the Bible's context, *'ebed* is better translated in many instances as "bondservant," which is similar to an indentured servant. A person became an indentured servant usually because they owed a debt they could not repay through their limited financial means. Rather than going to prison or suffering some other (usually worse) penalty, a person would "sell himself" to an *'adon* in Hebrew, a "boss" or employer. This word is sometimes translated as "master," but again, that is too strong a term in the context of indentured servitude.[5] When one person "purchases," "acquires," or "possesses" another person under the Mosaic law, it usually results from their voluntary servitude. The 'adon doesn't literally own the servant as much as the 'adon owns the servant's debt and obligation to work it off. Paul Copan and Robertson McQuilkin offer a modern-day analogy to which the biblical regulation of the acquiring of servants can be compared. Just as the "owners" of sports teams today "acquire" players for their teams and "own" their service on the field, so the 'adon of ancient Israel would acquire an 'ebed. The implication that these slaves are "subhuman property" is not what the word conveys in this context.

And yet the Bible does refer in some instances to an 'ebed as a person who has been forced into servitude as another's property (see, for example, Exodus 1:13, where Pharaoh and the Egyptians "ruthlessly made the people of Israel work as slaves"). While the Bible recognized the existence of such slavery in the ancient Near East, it didn't condone it. Indeed, the entire Exodus story is about God breaking the bonds of such slavery. Because of what God did to end involuntary servitude, the Israelites were commanded to treat voluntary servants and those captured after war with dignity and respect.[6] God's call for the Israelites to remember the bitterness of their former bondage even as they came to know freedom shapes how they treat those still in bondage and forms the backdrop against which we should view the Mosaic laws on servitude.

One might still remain skeptical and feel that these attempts at clarifying interpretation are nothing more than efforts to sidestep or explain away morally troubling passages of the Bible. The very words of Scripture, however, demonstrate that voluntary indentured servitude is what the Bible regulates within the Mosaic law of the Old Testament. "If your brother becomes poor beside you and sells himself to you," the Bible reads, "you shall not make him serve as a slave: he shall be with you as a hired worker and as a sojourner" (Lev. 25:39–40). The Mosaic law provides that such servitude is to be *temporary*: "When you buy a Hebrew slave [*'ebed*, or servant], he shall serve six years, and in the seventh he shall go out free, *for nothing*" (Ex. 21:2, emphasis added; cf. Deut. 15:12–18). Add to this the fact that masters were to provide freed servants with the means to start a debt-free life, and we see a biblical system for ending the cycle of poverty that would lead to servitude in the first place (Deut. 15:13–14). This is critical to grasping the chasm between biblical servitude and the chattel slavery practiced in the transatlantic slave trade. Every seventh year, whether the servant worked off the debt or not, they were to be freed of their obligations. In fact, the Bible goes a step further to ensure servitude's impermanence. Servants of every kind, regardless of whether they served six years or just six days, were to be released across the entirety of Israel every fifty years in the "year of Jubilee," a year in which Israel was to "proclaim liberty throughout the land to all its inhabitants"—again in remembrance of their own liberation from bondage (Lev. 25:10, 39–43). In the rare instance in which servitude was lifelong, it was only so voluntarily (Ex. 21:5–6). On this basis alone, biblical servitude stands in stark distinction to the slavery practiced as part of the transatlantic slave trade.

Widening the chasm of that distinction is the fact that biblical servitude was never meant to be institutionalized. In fact, simply practicing the biblical laws correctly would likely have led to servitude's abolition. "Israel had laws to mitigate poverty—and thus servitude—and controls to prevent institutionalizing it; these included gleaning laws, six-year service limits, the year of Jubilee, warnings to look out for 'the stranger, the orphan, and the widow who are in your midst' (Deut. 16:11), no-interest loans (Ex. 22:25), commands to lend freely to the poor (Deut. 15:7–8), and so on."[7]

Let us linger on these provisions for a moment in light of today's arguments that racial inequities persist in the West today because of social and legal structures. The Bible specifically sets forth principles that would limit inequities and eventually do away with servitude. If we applied these principles in some form to our modern social and legal structures, we might see that poverty, predatory lending, and similar conditions that have led to racial disparities could actually be mitigated. To be clear, I am not advocating a return to Old Testament law as the law of the land. Those laws pertained to and were applied in a context very different from what we experience today. Yet the wisdom and principles behind these ancient laws may serve to guide us in formulating policies for today's challenges. And yet the Bible is blamed for the modern inequities that the Christian Scriptures sought to minimize—if not completely eliminate.

The institutionalized transatlantic slave trade supplied slaves through brutality and kidnapping. Ripped from their families and homes, Africans were forcibly shipped overseas, subject to detestable conditions on crowded and disease-ridden ships, only to be put in shackles in a foreign land if they happened to survive their transport. Biblical servitude laws could not be more different in this regard. The Bible expressly prohibits kidnapping a person to sell or acquire as a slave. In fact, this is such a serious crime that it carries the death penalty (Deut. 24:7). "Whoever steals a man and sells him, and anyone found in possession of him," Exodus 21:16 demands, "shall be put to death."

In the transatlantic slave trade, masters could physically abuse their slaves with impunity. The Bible prohibits such evil. If a master struck a servant such that the servant died within a day or two, the slave would "be avenged," which is to say that the master would be executed (Ex. 21:20). To answer a possible objection here, the passage does provide that the slave will not "be avenged" if he dies after a day or two. Why this caveat? As Copan explains, "The master was given the benefit of the doubt that the servant was likely being disciplined and that there was no murderous intent. Of course, if the slave died immediately, no further proof was needed."[8] And in the case of harsh physical discipline that came short of killing a servant, the Bible mandates that the servant be released, free of his or her debts (Ex. 21:23–27). In other words, if a master strikes a servant severely enough to kill, the master risks forfeiting his own life. And if he strikes the servant hard enough to cause serious injury, he risks forfeiting his means of debt repayment and the servant goes free. Nothing like these safeguards against abuse existed in the transatlantic slave trade.

In the pre-Civil War American South, the Fugitive Slave Law required runaway slaves to be returned to their masters and prohibited anyone from harboring escaped slaves. Interestingly, ancient Near Eastern legal codes contemporary with the Bible also required the return of runaway slaves and imposed either harsh fines or the death penalty on violators.[9] Yet the Mosaic law required the exact opposite. It commanded Israelites to let runaway slaves live with them *in a place of the runaway's choosing* (Deut. 23:15–16). This is the kind of passage that inspired The Underground Railroad through which slaves fleeing their captors in the American South could find freedom in the American North. This passage of the Bible prohibiting the return of runaway slaves is clearly different from Southern antebellum laws *requiring* the return of captured slaves and subjecting those who harbored runaway slaves to the death penalty.

It's a night-and-day difference. When paired with the Bible's death penalty for kidnapping slaves, the contrast is more evident yet.

Let's pause here for a moment to recognize not only the Bible's contrast to the antebellum southern slave trade, but also the lie that the Bible exposes here. We know that proslavery advocates invoked the Bible to justify this abominable practice. Yet they enacted laws, like the Fugitive Slave Law, that expressly contradict the Bible. In fact, the Fugitive Slave Law mimics not the Bible, but the legal codes of Israel's pagan neighbors! One cannot but lament over the soul-selling needed to justify antebellum slavery for a person calling himself a Christian.

Allow me to take a bold stance here. Even when slavery ended in the United States, it did so deficiently. After the Civil War, in what was called Reconstruction, slaves were free, but only free *from* their captors. They were not set free *for* a promising future. By and large, they had the shirts on their backs, likely very little money, and not much else. They had no land to farm, no money to invest, not even a map to tell them where to go. They were left on their own, like settlers in a land that had already been settled but with fewer supplies. While emancipation was, indeed, a tremendous victory, the plights of the newly freed slaves were not vastly improved. Yes, they were liberated, but liberated to a wilderness in which much of the land had already been claimed and built upon. This tilled the soil for predatory practices that effectively reenslaved African Americans. W. E. B. Du Bois said of this period, "The slave went free, stood a brief moment in the sun, then moved back again toward slavery."[10] I believe the later plight of these newly freed slaves could have been avoided had we let biblical principles guide us more thoroughly.

Perhaps a different future would have resulted had we consulted Scripture's guidance on how to establish someone with a chance for success. In the context of indentured servitude, the Bible provides that servants released from their obligations were to be given provisions for a fresh start. "And when you let him go free from you, you shall not let him go empty-handed. You shall furnish him liberally out of your flock, out of your threshing floor, and out of your winepress. As the LORD your God has blessed you, you shall give to him" (Deut. 15:13–14). With this command in view, an *'adon*, or "master," within Israel might carefully consider whether being an *'adon* would be worth it in the first place. And if he did, he had every incentive to make sure that his servants were treated well so that the *'adon's* flocks, threshing floors, and winepresses yielded enough to liberally be given to the released servant and still leave enough for the *'adon's* family. But the more profound effect is that the servant is freed with enough to start a debt-free life—with a minimal chance of returning to debt servitude.[11] Perhaps this is why Jacob Milgrom alluded to Deuteronomy 15:12–15 as a passage that "virtually abolishes the institution of slavery."[12]

The structure of biblical laws that would regulate indentured servitude out of existence provides yet another contrast to the laws of the transatlantic slave trade, whose profiteers sought to perpetuate at every turn. Steeped in realism and providing an accurate diagnosis of the human condition, the Bible regulates servitude without condoning it. The cultures surrounding the Israelites practiced *both* chattel slavery and indentured servitude. The Bible provides regulations standing against the former and limiting the latter. Debt servitude wasn't ideal, but it was a reality of the time due to economic conditions, scarce resources, and the harsh realities of war. The biblical laws mitigated these harsh realities without lauding servitude as a social or economic good. That's why the Mosaic law—which contains the regulations on servitude—repeatedly reminded the Israelites of their former slavery in Egypt. They were never to forget that servitude, whether voluntary or involuntary, temporary or lifelong, is not what God intended.

We see the juxtaposition of the moral ideal against the less-than-moral reality in the New Testament as well. The Pharisees approached Jesus to test him, asking, "Is it lawful to divorce one's wife for any cause?" Jesus replied by pointing to the unity of marriage. "What therefore God has joined together, let not man separate." Puzzled by this, the Pharisees referenced the Mosaic law that allowed for divorce. "Why then did Moses command one to give a certificate of divorce and to send her away?" In their simplistic view, whatever the Bible regulates it also condones. But Jesus pointed out that the regulations were *not approvals but indictments* of the human heart and efforts to mitigate the damage. "Because of your hardness of heart," Jesus responded, "Moses allowed you to divorce your wives, but from the beginning it was not so. And I say to you: whoever divorces his wife, except for sexual immorality, and marries another, commits adultery" (Matt. 19:1–9). Legal sanction doesn't always mean approval.

THE NEW COVENANT AGAINST SLAVERY

In the New Testament age, Roman slavery *was* a system of chattel (property) slavery unlike the debt servitude regulated in the Old Testament. But it is important to keep in mind that like the Hebrew word *'ebed*, the New Testament Greek word *doulos* can sometimes mean "bondservant" in the sense of voluntary servitude, and it can mean "slave" in the sense of involuntary servitude. Other times the word is meant to convey slavery in a spiritual sense. The translators of the English Standard Version of the Bible point this out in explaining their translation philosophy: "Where absolute owner-ship by a master is envisaged (as in Romans 6), 'slave' is used; where a more limited form of servitude is in view, 'bondservant' is used (as in 1 Corinthians 7:21–24); where the context indicates a wide range of freedom (as in John 4:51), 'servant' is preferred."[13] This accounts for why it may seem that neither Jesus nor Paul nor any of the other New Testament authors expressly condemn slavery in every instance that the word *doulos* appears in the New Testament. The condemnation does not follow every instance of *doulos* because not every instance of *doulos* refers to chattel slavery. When it does, however, we see both explicit condemnations of the practice and implicit encouragements for slave owners to repent of it.

DEALING WITH THE REALITY BY APPEALING TO THE HEART

Paul declared that slaves are just as equal in Christ to their masters (Gal. 3:28). And yet, some might argue, in 1 Corinthians 7:21–22, Paul seemed to encourage slaves who become Christians to remain in their state of slavery and settle for a form of spiritual freedom: "Were you a slave when you were called? Don't let it trouble you. . . . For the one who was a slave when called to faith in the Lord is the Lord's freed person" (NIV). Slavers of the past used this passage to try to pacify African slaves who became Christians to be satisfied with a spiritual freedom and resign themselves to their physical bondage. Such a manipulation was (and is) the height of dishonesty. They cherry-picked the passage, plucking its words out of context and concealing key phrases.

The entirety of the passage shows that Paul *encouraged* slaves to seek their physical freedom and warned those who might find themselves in a position to become bondservants to avoid it at all costs. The entirety of the passage reads, "Were you a slave when you were called? Don't let it trouble you—*although if you can gain your freedom, do so.* For the one who was a slave when called to faith in the Lord is the Lord's freed person; similarly, the one who was free when called is Christ's slave. You were bought at a price; *do not become slaves of human beings*" (1 Cor. 7:21–23 NIV, emphasis added). When we drink this passage in fully, we see that it radically departs from Roman law and the slave culture it fostered. As Esau McCaulley points out, Paul's first letter to the Corinthians was meant to be read by and to slaves and masters alike.[14] Paul worded this somewhat surreptitiously because the fledgling Christian movement had little power to change the Roman political machine and risked being crushed for infighting treason.

The masters of the transatlantic slave trade evaded the broader context of Paul's message. Starting in 1 Corinthians 7:17, Paul said that those who become Christians should not try to change their social status, especially as it pertains to religious piety and tradition. "Each person should remain in the situation they were in when God called them," he wrote (v. 20 NIV). Paul recommended that believers try to remain unmarried or married, betrothed or unbetrothed, depending on their status before becoming Christians (1 Cor. 7:25–35). Amid those verses, jutting out like a mountain on a prairie, Paul took the opposite approach regarding the status of slaves. He encouraged them *not* to stay that way and instead find their freedom. He told masters to see slaves as their equals. This contrast alone punctuates the Bible's declaration that slavery was an immoral state for humanity.

The equality of servants and masters hearkens back to the Old Testament, including one of its most ancient books, the book of Job. There Job asked,

> If I have denied justice to any of my servants,
>> whether male or female,
>> when they had a grievance against me,
> what will I do when God confronts me?
>> What will I answer when called to account?
>> Did not he who made me in the womb make them?
>> Did not the same one form us both within our
>>> mothers?"

Job 31:13–15 NIV

The entire corpus of Scripture, from beginning to end, proclaims that all are equal and that no one is to be denied equal justice.

Through this lens, we can properly read what Paul was communicating in 1 Timothy 6:1–3, where he appears to have told "all who are under the yoke of slavery" (NIV) to respect their masters. First, the words "yoke of slavery" can be translated as "yoke as bondservants" (ESV), meaning that this is a voluntary, indentured servitude and not chattel slavery. Nevertheless, in light of 1 Corinthians 7:21, it is evident that Paul was encouraging those who found themselves in servitude to live out their faith in the midst of undesirable circumstances because "even in slavery one has an ability to live in a way that testifies to their beliefs."[15] Slaves were not the mere tools that society often saw them to be. Though robbed of their freedom, they were not robbed of their influence.

This understanding makes sense given that at the beginning of that same letter, Paul condemned "slave traders" as sinners

(1 Tim. 1:9–10 NIV). This condemnation went beyond Paul. In Revelation 18:13 "John condemns 'Babylon' (ancient Rome; cf. 1 Peter 5:13) for her trafficking in humans as cargo ('bodies and souls of humans'—or 'bodies, that is, the souls of humans')."[16] These are not isolated needles of protest in the haystack of the New Testament. We will soon see that Jesus, in word and in deed, opposed human inequality—especially when based on ethnicity. It was his words, his actions, indeed his very life that inspired not only the politically unconnected New Testament authors to quietly oppose slavery but also the politically influential abolitionists to put a stop to it.

NOT A MATTER OF COLOR

Slavery advocates had to stretch and twist the Bible quite a bit to force it into the racially charged mold they desired. They rested primarily on the so-called curse of Ham, found in Genesis 9:25–27. The context is that Ham, Noah's youngest son, found him drunk, asleep, and naked. Instead of covering his father, he told his older brothers, Shem and Japheth. They took care not to look on their father's nakedness as they covered him back up. Upon discovering what Ham had done, Noah became incensed and pronounced this curse on Ham's son, Canaan:

> "Cursed be Canaan!
>> The lowest of slaves
>> will he be to his brothers."

He also said,

"Praise be to the LORD, the God of Shem!
    May Canaan be the slave of Shem.
May God extend Japheth's territory;
        may Japheth live in the tents of Shem,
        and may Canaan be the slave of Japheth."
    (NIV)

As the slaveholder's interpretation goes, God cursed Ham and his family to be slaves marked by black skin, since the name Ham is related to the Hebrew word for black, and Africans are descended from Ham's son Canaan. This interpretation found its way into pre-Civil War era Christian circles and even persisted in the footnotes of the 1917 *Scofield Bible*.

Those interpretations aren't right. In fact, they don't even rise to the level of being wrong.

First and most obvious is the fact that Noah pronounced the curse, not God. Thus, there is no "divine decree" that curses all of Ham's offspring. Second, the curse was leveled toward Canaan, Ham's son, not Ham himself. Further, according to many biblical scholars, Canaan isn't the only progenitor of Africans. Cush, Mizraim, and Put, Ham's other—non-cursed—sons were also. Biblically speaking, Cush was the forefather of the Nubians (modern Sudanese) and Ethiopians, while Mizraim and Put were the progenitors of Egypt and Libya, respectively. Ham's descendants, on the other hand, cover a spectrum of colors across the Middle East and Africa and beyond (including Egyptians, Babylonians, and Philistines: people known more for being oppressors and enslavers in the Old Testament rather than being oppressed and enslaved themselves). DNA analyses have shown that more than 90 percent of modern Lebanese peoples share their genes with the ancient Canaanites.[17] Third, the curse was fulfilled with Joshua's conquest of Canaan, the people named after Ham's son. Joshua is a descendent of Shem, one of the brothers Canaan was told he would serve. Fourth, as David Goldenberg has convincingly shown, the words for "Ham" and "black" are *not* related etymologically. This is a later development that he traces back to between the second and fourth centuries.[18] In other words, the one cursed is not the one with black-skinned descendants.

Slavery's advocates knew this legion of problems with their theory. Indeed, many abolitionists pressed these problems in opposing them. Alas, ignorance of the Bible wasn't the problem. Greed, apathy, and willful misinterpretation were.[19]

Western Europeans relied on the "curse of Ham" when the Spanish and Portuguese enslaved dark-skinned peoples in the fifteenth century. By the early colonial period, though, a fully racialized version of the "curse of Ham" had made its way to America.[20] David Brion Davis, one of the foremost experts in New World slavery, sees the evident Scripture twisting. Genesis 9 "was not an originally racist biblical script that led to the enslavement of 'Ham's black descendants,' but rather [it was] the increasing enslavement of blacks that transformed biblical interpretation."[21] The fact that proslavery advocates had to rely on such spurious interpretations exposes just how difficult it is to enlist the Bible's aid to justify race-based chattel slavery.

SLAVERY OF NON-ISRAELITES?

Now, there are some passages that, if not properly interpreted, appear to condone the acquisition and ownership of people *outside* of the Israelites as chattel slaves. In other words, one might interpret the Bible as condoning ethnicity-based chattel slavery. For example, "Leviticus 25 seems to allow a person to 'acquire male and female slaves from the pagan nations that are around you. . . . Then, too, it is out of the sons of the sojourners who live as aliens among you that you may acquire, and out of their families who are with you, whom they will have produced in your land; they also may become your possession. You may even bequeath them to your sons after you, to receive as a possession; you can use them as permanent slaves (Lev. 25:44–46).'"[22] Taking this passage in isolation might lead one to believe that—contrary to what I have been saying to this point—the Bible condones chattel slavery of non-Israelites, a form of race-based chattel slavery. But such an out-of-context interpretation would not only be erroneous but unfair.

Just as a judge must interpret a statutory clause in light of the statute's surrounding context, we, too, must look at this passage in the surrounding context of the Bible's regulation of servitude. "Earlier in Leviticus, Israel was commanded to love the stranger in the land just as one loved the native. Such passages set a tone for some of the more difficult-to-interpret-texts."[23] As we've already seen, the verb "acquire" (*qānāh*) does not necessarily mean "acquire as property." It can mean "acquire rights of authority." One who follows sports will readily think of language in which a particular team "acquires" a player, such as when the Chicago Bulls "acquired" Dennis Rodman from the Detroit Pistons.

Further, there is nothing that precludes the Bible's regulations on servitude (as opposed to slavery) for Israelites to applying identically to non-Israelite servants. In fact, other areas of the Bible mandate that Israelites treat foreigners as equals (see Ex. 23:9; Lev. 19:33–34; 24:22; Num. 15:15–16). "In light of Leviticus 25's context and in consideration of other relevant passages," McQuilkin and Copan write, "why couldn't the conditions for acquiring foreign 'slaves' be *identical* to acquiring Israelite servants—namely, *extreme poverty and voluntarily attaching themselves to an Israelite household*?"[24] There's no reason why not. In fact, Leviticus 25:47 allows a "stranger" or "sojourner" among the Israelites (i.e., a foreigner) to pay his way out of his debt servitude if he gains the financial ability to do so. Would it be difficult for such a servant to become rich enough to do that? Of course. But the biblical law recognizes that possibility for Hebrew servants in the same context as its discussion about foreigners growing their wealth among the Israelites (v. 49).

These biblical provisions regarding servitude of foreigners are actually remarkable, compared not only to laws of modern, race-based slavery, but also to the institutionalized slavery of other ancient Near Eastern cultures. The Code of Hammurabi, for example, permitted lifelong, involuntary slavery either through prisoners of war or kidnapping.[25] Hammurabi's Code also mandated that runaway slaves be returned to their owners under penalty of death, while other codes imposed heavy fines.[26] Owners could physically abuse, even kill, their slaves and break up their families by selling them off separately to new owners. Similarly barbarous laws existed in other ancient Near Eastern codes as well.[27] Comparing these codes with the laws and practices of the transatlantic slave trade is like looking at a pair of matching shoes. Comparing those ancient codes with the biblical texts is like trying to wear a sandal with a stiletto-heeled shoe.

Ancient Near Eastern slavery, coupled with harsh realities of poverty, scarce resources, and constant war form the context for biblical laws on servitude, especially servitude of non-Israelites. In stark contrast to the other codes, the Bible sought to mitigate the suffering and even allow for foreigners to earn a living, stay with their families, and perhaps even buy their way out of servitude. The Bible not only addresses the harsh realities non-Israelites faced; it sought to end them and provide a hope for a future.

Some may argue that ethnic superiority is at least implied in the Bible given that God commands the Israelites to kill all the Canaanites and Amalekites, including women and children, so that the Israelites may possess the land (Deut. 20:16–18; Josh. 10:40; 1 Sam. 15:3). Critics have called the biblical episode in which this occurred "the Canaanite genocide" or, as Richard Dawkins has put it, "ethnic cleansing." Space doesn't permit a detailed treatment of how these commands were *not* about ethnic superiority or about genocide.[28] Suffice it to say here that labeling these commands as genocide is, frankly, a prejudicial simplification. God commands the Israelites to wipe out the Canaanites and Amalekites not because of their genetic differences (the differences were minimal anyway), but because of the Canaanite immorality. Canaanites practiced temple prostitution, chattel slavery, marauding, idolatry, and child sacrifice (cf. Lev. 18:20–30; Deut. 9:4–6). The Amalekites were bent on Israel's destruction (Judg. 3:13; 6:3–5, 33; 7:12). The better term would be *judgment* rather than genocide. In fact, the command to wipe out the Canaanites is more properly viewed as a command to eliminate their way of life, which was based on and steeped in atrocities. Their practices—not their races or ethnicities—were the impetus for God's command to wipe out the Canaanites.[29] How can we be sure that race and ethnicity played no role in these commands? The fact that God warned Israel herself that if she should succumb to such immorality she would be judged just as harshly, perhaps even more so (2 Kings 17:7–41; 2 Chron. 36:15–21; Jer. 1). God made good on that warning, using foreign powers to judge Israel when the nation participated in detestable practices.

Slavery itself is a poison. Chattel slavery is like adding cyanide to arsenic. Race-based chattel slavery is a cocktail of cyanide, arsenic, and ricin. Slavery not based on race devastates people because of their socioeconomic status. Race-based chattel slavery—and by extension all expressions of racism—is even more corrosive because it degrades victims based on who they are, not the circumstances they find themselves in. Circumstances can be changed (though with tremendous difficulty). But one's race is an immutable characteristic. Racism takes an important facet of our identities and labels it as a defect of character and ontology. Even murder, as awful as it is, takes a life usually because of what the victim has that the murderer wants. Racism, by contrast, plunders a victim because of who the victim is. The biblical laws progressively sought to end such plunder. The life of Jesus, the one in whom the law was fulfilled, exemplified for us what it takes to achieve that.

THEY SAW THE DIFFERENCE

An undercurrent flowed during the entirety of the slave trade—one that gnawed at the consciences of those who would call themselves Christians. That undercurrent was the Word of God itself. As Carl Ellis Jr. has said, it is a historical mistake to conclude that Christianity was imposed on unwilling Africans through the institution of race-based slavery as a means of pacifying slaves. In fact, slave masters resisted Christianizing slaves because introducing this religion, the fundamental tenets of which teach that every human is endowed with God's image (Gen. 1:26–27) and that freedom is humanity's ultimate destiny (John 8:36; Gal. 5:13), to them was a little too risky.

Indeed, Ron Behm and Columbus Salley point out that at first Christianity was a *barrier* to race-based slavery because there was a tradition that a Christian could not be held as a slave by another Christian. The thinking was that if Africans were allowed to convert to Christianity, they could no longer be held as slaves. "Baptism would be tantamount to emancipation."[30] To get around this inconvenient truth, slave masters and traders passed a series of laws between 1667 and 1671 dictating that conversion did not release someone from servitude. The mental gymnastics were many, it seems, as the Church of England and various American colonies came to the conclusion that Christianity was compatible with slavery. It wasn't just lawmakers and monarchs who came to such wrongheaded conclusions. Unfortunately, otherwise brilliant Christian theologians compromised the Scriptures to justify their complicity in one of the worst evils in human history.[31]

Slaves of African descent saw through the subterfuge, machinations, and bad interpretations. The more I study the life and words of former slave Frederick Douglass, the more inspired I am by the man's intellect, eloquence, and bravery. One needs only to read Douglass's speech, "What to the Slave Is the Fourth of July?" to be convinced that he was mentally blessed in abundant measure. He spoke not as one showing off his gifts (I'm quite certain Douglass knew how intelligent he was), but as someone who refused to lower the moral and intellectual bar. By calling all of us to higher standards, he encouraged us to rise. That's a picture painted with the brush of irony, isn't it? Frederick Douglass, a slave who managed to rise from a wretched plight and advocate for the disenfranchised, encouraged those in lofty positions to climb out of their states of wretched comfort so that all of us, with the help of God, could strive toward a pinnacle of moral harmony.

Douglass saw past the slavers' distortions of Scripture with a clear enough lens to see Jesus for who he really is. He wrote,

> Between the Christianity of this land, and the Christianity of Christ, I recognize the widest possible difference—so wide, that to receive the one as good, pure, and holy, is of necessity to be the enemy of the other. I love the pure, peaceable, and impartial Christianity of Christ: I therefore hate the corrupt, slaveholding, women-whipping, cradle-plundering, partial and hypocritical Christianity of this land. . . . Indeed, I can see no reason, but the most deceitful one, for calling the religion of this land Christianity.[32]

Douglass saw in the authentic teaching and life of Christ how counterfeit the Christianity of racists was.

Weeks after the young African American man and I wrestled over some tough issues, I had the joy of receiving a letter from him, telling me that he was on a journey of rediscovering faith. Perhaps he began to see what Douglass saw—"the pure, peaceable, and impartial Christianity of Christ." Let's gaze upon that Christ now.

CHAPTER 5

JESUS AND AUTHENTIC ETHNIC EQUALITY

CAMEL JOCKEY

The strip mall pizza shop's windows mirrored the flow of traffic behind me as I stood just outside, enjoying a slice of the pizza my younger brother, cousin, and I had just purchased (pizza seems to be a part of important moments for me). We were using a flat-topped trash can just beyond the shop's door as our dinner table because, like most boys around eleven years old, our sense of sanitation was alarmingly deficient. My deepest thought at that moment was likely something like, "Wow, this glass is like a mirror; I can see everything behind me." But then my eyes caught something just beyond the glass's reflection. I saw the eighteen-year-old pizza shop employee who had just given us our pizza. His eyes were fixed on me, full of contempt. He had raised his hand just slightly higher than his head to make sure I didn't miss his protruding middle finger.

For some reason, despite the fact that he was seven years older than me, I went inside the shop. I don't think I went in to confront him. I don't think I went in to see if I had offended him in some way. My body just moved automatically, reacting from pure shock. "Is that middle finger for me?" I asked in an adrenaline-shaken voice.

"That's right, camel jockey," he barked back. "What are you going to do about it?"

My shock at the gesture was replaced by trauma at the ethnic assault. His face projected a churning contempt coupled with a scary eagerness. He was hoping I would say something back to escalate the conflict. I can't imagine what he thought would happen. Would he come from behind the counter to fight with me? Would he just start yelling epithets in front of his coworkers? To this day, that encounter mystifies me.

As I walked out, I likely muttered an anemic comeback, to which he blathered, "That's what I thought. Now go back to where you came from, *sand n—*," or something similarly ignorant (I was born in America) and horrible (the last slur efficiently denigrated two ethnicities at the same time).

For whatever reason, he had tried to rob me of my dignity. And for the next twenty-four hours, it seemed he was succeeding. All I could think about was the look in his eyes as he leveled the insult. It was not the last time "camel jockey" or "sand n—" or "rag head" would be thrown my way. But that pizza shop experience was my first bitter morsel of the pain of prejudice. Thirty-seven years have passed since that day. Yet on the rare occasion I drive by that shop, the acid creeps up my throat, reminding me. I endured but a bite, perhaps nothing more than a taste, of the hate others have endured because of their ethnicities. Yet the aftertaste has lingered with me.

THE TESTS OF OUR TIME

Events of the past ten years have heightened our sensitivities and our emotions about racial justice. Fiery demands for justice have been met with equally fiery denials that injustice has occurred. The resultant smoke and cacophony have watered our eyes so that we cannot see and assaulted our ears so that we cannot hear the gospel's call for all to see their equal value. Some have equated Christian voices with political voices, with voices that speak almost entirely on one side of divisive issues. While Christians shouldn't be silent on political matters, the reality is that our decibels on that which is political overpower our decibels on that which is spiritual. In our exchanges on racial justice, we often get caught up in debating whether racial injustice exists systemically, resulting in the gospel message getting lost in the fray.

This is tragic because the gospel message is one of hope and of powerful lament. Coupling lament over real problems with hope for the future clears a pathway to solutions and healing. God not only calls us to weep over injustice but actually weeps over it himself. The Bible's shortest verse recounts that "Jesus wept" (John 11:35). He wept alongside the family of his recently dead friend, Lazarus. Lazarus was not a man of political import or national significance. He was just a local guy. Yet in Charles Spurgeon's words, "Our Saviour wept in *sympathy with domestic sorrow*, and sanctified the tears of the bereaved."[1] We need to weep alongside individuals and local communities directly affected by the hatred, violence, and even apathy that give substance to racial and ethnic prejudice. Middle Eastern, community-oriented Jesus wept in a domestic sorrow.

Jesus also lamented on a national scale. He wept over his beloved Jerusalem because it was embroiled in a calamity of its own making.

"When he drew near and saw the city, he wept over it, saying, 'Would that you, even you, had known on this day the things that make for peace! But now they are hidden from your eyes" (Luke 19:41–42). Jesus' words are hauntingly pertinent today. We seem to be ignorant—whether willfully or otherwise—of the things that would bring us peace. Our desire to be right, to be justified, to think of "us" more than "them," hides these things from our eyes. And so we suffer collectively, some racial and ethnic groups more than others, because hatred simply doesn't have anything that makes for peace. As Spurgeon pointed out, "Our Lord, in weeping over Jerusalem, showed his *sympathy with national troubles*, his distress at the evils which awaited his countrymen. Men should not cease to be patriots when they become believers; saints should bemoan the ills which come upon the guilty people among whom they are numbered, and do so all the more because they are saints."[2]

Jesus lamented over domestic tragedies, and he lamented over national tragedies. If we allow the biblical themes of local and national equality to surprise us once again, just as they surprised Jesus' Middle Eastern audiences, perhaps we can learn to lament domestically and nationally once more.

Why did Jesus weep over the domestic tragedy of his friend Lazarus's death? He was just about to raise Lazarus from the dead, after all. He lamented because Lazarus's death was a reminder that the tragedies that befall humanity are not what God originally intended. God created us for harmonious relationship with himself. But the world has fallen away from that intention, and so we suffer the indignities of death and racism. As he wept over Lazarus, Jesus mourned over the past, at how we lost the blessing of what was intended. Jesus saw the present suffering. But he was confident in a brighter future, one that would lead to resurrection and life.

Yet Jesus still wept. He wept over the death of one person, Lazarus, and he wept over the wounds of a nation. I have no doubt that Jesus lamented the hatred I experienced as an eleven-year-old boy just as he laments every act of racism. I also have no doubt that Jesus laments the national and even global scourge of racism, whether individual or systemic. Yet just as he followed his lament for Lazarus with a miracle, our laments over racism can be trailed by hope. Indeed, the biblical progression is that hope always follows lament.

I have had the blessing of seeing the gospel's hope displayed following lament over racial tensions. Some years before George Floyd's death captured the world's attention and outrage, the killings of four African American men—Trayvon Martin, Eric Garner, Michael Brown, and Tamir Rice—made American headlines. Their deaths loaded the powder keg about police use of force on ethnic minorities that would eventually explode when Floyd was killed. In reaction to those earlier deaths, I found myself huddled in prayer with multiethnic faith leaders in Detroit. In just a few minutes, we would be on stage speaking into microphones about the gospel's role in racial reconciliation. There I was, clasping hands with Latino, black, Arab, Jewish, and white preachers and leaders. Just the sight of that was enough to quiver the lip and flood the eyes.

But uncertainty hung in the room. Across the country tensions were flaring, slogans were being created, and lines were being drawn. Having felt the sting of racial division so powerfully in 1968, Detroit was especially sensitive to the rising tension. As we prayed, none of us knew how many people might attend the event. None of us knew whether there would be handshakes or shaking fists.

I walked into the large auditorium and saw only a few islands of people scattered amid the sea of seats. As I removed the "reserved" sign from my front-row seat, I chuckled at the optimism that led someone to reserve any seats that night. I sat down and bowed my head in prayer.

Minutes later the master of ceremonies approached the microphone. After he introduced the speakers, surprisingly thunderous applause wrenched my head upright. How could so few make so much noise? Walking onto the stage, I saw that multicolored faces filled the auditorium. How so many had silently gathered into that place without my noticing remains a bit of a mystery.

The evening was amazing. There was diversity on the stage and in the crowd. And there was diversity of perspectives on the controversies. Yet there was unity of belief.

The audience asked challenging, passionate, yet congenial questions. Afterward they lingered in the foyer for nearly two hours, engaging one another on the issues. Smiles were everywhere, handshakes and hugs were common, and prayer was pervasive. The gospel had united us for just an evening in just one building.

Common belief, as I've already argued, isn't enough to completely unite us and bring racial reconciliation. I mention this because despite the gospel's influence in ending the slave trade and apartheid, and in bringing about civil rights reform, it is often said that Sunday morning remains the most segregated time in America.[3] In the years since that meeting, there have been similar such events, and many have turned out well. The polarization of Western society has kept pace with faith-based racial reconciliation efforts, however. In some ways, it has outpaced it, because polarization is easy while reconciliation is difficult. Polarization happens automatically in two ways. I recently watched a documentary titled *The Social Dilemma*, produced by several founding members of the world's most influential social media platforms. They shared that what started out as innocent ways to bring people with common interests together has evolved into algorithms that cloister us into tribes with similar hobbies, convictions, voting allegiances, and thought worlds. Eventually we come to think of anyone who disagrees with us as either an oddball or a social menace. This mathematical polarization plays to our baser instincts of tribalism, groupthink, and vilification. And so polarization and division technologically outpace reconciliation at a geometric rate.

Jesus was no stranger to polarization. And ethnic discrimination and segregation weren't foreign to Jesus' culture even (and sometimes especially) among people of the same religion. Jews and Samaritans had similar religions, yet they were deeply divided ethnically. In the church's earliest days, there was division between Jewish and Gentile Christians. Jesus' words and deeds had made such continued hostility and division unthinkable. He often confronted the religious authorities and cultural beliefs of his day over this very issue—and he did so with mastery. That mastery was displayed when he balanced the paradox of respecting his traditional communal Middle Eastern culture while challenging its intractable groupthink.

JONAH OR PETER?
WHO WILL WE CHOOSE TO BE?

Before Jesus walked the streets of Galilee and Jerusalem, God had been signaling his equal regard for all of humanity and challenging people to get beyond their tribalism and groupthink. In fact, God has been telling humans this since the beginning, weaving a thread of unity and equality throughout the tapestry of history.

The Bible opens by recounting God's creation of the universe and everything in it. Genesis 2 details the creation of humanity from the original couple, Adam and Eve. This is a familiar story, but we mustn't let our familiarity obscure something significant. Other ancient Near Eastern creation accounts detail the gods and lesser gods fighting with each other and struggling to subdue the elements to create the world. Humanity's creation seems almost an afterthought and usually for the purpose of creating slaves for manual labor. The biblical narrative, on the other hand, describes one God who has no rival and needs not subdue the elements of creation, but brings them into existence. More to the point, whereas myths account for human creation as a sidebar, the Bible depicts God's special and interactive creation of humanity. Philosopher William Lane Craig describes these differences and points out a question Old Testament scholars have wrestled with. "Why doesn't the Pentateuch [the first five books of the Bible] just begin with the call of Abraham in Genesis 12 and the founding of the nation of Israel?" Summing up the scholarly consensus, Craig says that it is because of "the universalizing interest of the author" who "wants to show that God's original plan was to bless all of mankind . . . not just his select people of Israel."[4] Amid the details of creation, the Bible defies the common claim that it is tribalistic and ethnically partial.

God's impartial love contrasts with the ethnic partialities of his own prophets who have to learn lessons about equality the hard way. Consider Jonah, a name the most unchurched person would know because of the story in which a giant sea creature swallows him. His story is far deeper than the sea from which the creature that swallowed him came. Jonah unhesitatingly delivered God's message to the people of Israel, but he balked when God asked him to change his ethnic audience. God told Jonah to warn the

Assyrian city of Nineveh that judgment was near unless the people turned from their violence. Jonah feared that the Ninevites would heed the warning and be saved from destruction. So rather than obey, Jonah fled in the opposite direction, going to Joppa to board a ship to Tarshish.

Jonah eventually obeyed God and warned the Ninevites. Just as he feared they would, they repented on a citywide scale. This bothered Jonah so much that he told God that he would rather die than live and see the wicked Assyrians forgiven by God. "That is why I made haste to flee to Tarshish; for I knew that you are a gracious God and merciful, slow to anger and abounding in steadfast love, and relenting from disaster" (Jonah 4:2). In his tantrum, Jonah expressed no remorse over his ethnic animosity toward the Ninevites. He saw no problem with juxtaposing his hatred with God's love. *The Ninevites deserve judgment for their evil, don't they? God is Israel's God, isn't he? Israelites are God's chosen, aren't they? The only people who should enjoy God's mercy are the Hebrews.* Jonah's ethnic antipathy blinded him from all logic. After all, mercy, by definition, is neither earned nor deserved. And so when Jonah implied that only the Israelites *deserved* God's mercy when they acted wickedly, Jonah sacrificed logic on the altar of prejudice. The very last line of the book of Jonah is a question from God to Jonah. "And should not I pity Nineveh, that great city, in which there are more than 120,000 persons who do not know their right hand from their left, and also much cattle?" Not only does this closing question expose Jonah's naked prejudice, but it also serves to make God's compassion for all ethnicities the punctuation mark that completes the book.

Centuries later God displayed his equal love for all people through the apostle Peter. Peter was a pious Jew, careful to observe the dietary laws that regulated Jewish life. In Acts 10:9–33, we read Peter's account of how God gave him a vision of a "great sheet descending, being let down by its four corners upon the earth" (v. 11). In that sheet were all kinds of animals, including animals forbidden for a Jew like Peter to eat. Yet God commanded Peter to eat those very animals (v. 13). Similar to Jonah before him, Peter at first refused God. "By no means, Lord," Peter retorted, "for I have never eaten anything that is common or unclean" (v. 14). But God responded, "What God has made clean, do not call common" (v. 15). Immediately after, God sent Peter to a Roman centurion named Cornelius. Cornelius and his entire household came to believe in Jesus. Peter was so excited about this that he reported it to the leaders of the nascent church, who all rejoiced: "To the Gentiles also God has granted repentance that leads to life" (Acts 11:18).

God's response to Peter's initial revulsion was short in length yet cavernous with meaning. The vision of the animals once forbidden to be eaten told Peter that Gentiles—non-Jews—are clean. Peter's objection to eating what God had commanded was that he had never eaten anything common (Gk., *koinon*) or unclean (Gk., *akatharton*). In the context, God wasn't merely talking about food; he was talking about relationships with others outside the Jews' ethnic boundaries. Like Jonah so many years before, Jews of Peter's day may have considered such people "common" or ritually "unclean." But they were no longer to be seen that way, especially in the light of Christ's having paid the price for the sins of the world, not just the Jews. That's why God's response to Peter remains so profound. "What God has made clean, do not call common" (Acts 10:15). Notice the order? Through Christ's atoning sacrifice, God has given all of us the opportunity to become clean. And why? Because we are not "common." Though there are and have been billions of people on the earth, not one of us is common. Each of us is sacred, having a unique sacredness as an individual human while at the same time having a corporate sacredness as members of the human family. Peter's hesitancy is transformed into joy as he excitedly tells leaders in the burgeoning church that God seeks the salvation of every race. Racism and xenophobia know of no such sublime concepts, and so they are morally and spiritually bankrupt philosophies.

Scripture surprises us with hidden rivets of detail that pull the material of God's Word to form a strong junction. Consider two such rivets: the common locations and common themes in Jonah's and Peter's stories. Jonah, who first resisted God's call to preach repentance to non-Jews, fled to Tarshish by way of Joppa. In Joppa Peter momentarily resisted but ultimately obeyed the revelation that the gospel should be preached to non-Jews. These rivets draw us to consider whether we approach the issue of race with Jonah's begrudging heart or Peter's joyful spirit.

Jonah obeyed the law (God's command to deliver his messages) when it came to ethnically different people. He knew of God's loving concern for people of all ethnicities, the very concern that was behind the command. But by failing to make room in his own heart for the spirit behind the law, Jonah remained bitter. This is the shortcoming in our approach to social justice that primarily seeks to change laws before changing hearts and minds. History shows that even when laws change for the better—and even when society changes positively in response—but there is no accompanying heart changes, bitterness and bile sit at the bottom of our hearts like sediment. Like Jonah, those whose hearts have not transformed along with the law come to resent the laws and the ones who implemented them. Changed laws riveted together with changed hearts can bind progress together. Neither is sufficient on its own, but both are necessary. The changes for the better in the Roman world, when the gospel message transformed the hearts of the people and the minds of the rulers, are testimony to the enduring bond that combines the law's spirit with the Spirit's transformation.

A SEED SOWN IN SAMARIA

I wonder if Peter's eager obedience to the vision he received was the fruit of seeds planted by Jesus' words and deeds on ethnic equality. John 4 gives us a rich account of such words and deeds. Jesus and the disciples made their way through Samaria—a region that was ethnically despised by Jews. They considered Samaritans to be ethnic half-breeds, a mix of Jew and Gentile, as well as theological compromisers. So as they entered the area filled with racial tensions, Jesus' disciples were likely wary of their surroundings, on their guards, waiting for ethnically driven confrontation. This two-thousand-year-old account sounds a little too familiar to our modern ears, does it not?

It's interesting that the Bible says that Jesus and the disciples "had" to go through Samaria. Logistically, they could have taken a path to avoid the region altogether. There's no indication that they were in a hurry, yet they took a shortcut through a hated area anyway. It's as if the narrative conveys that Jesus felt a compulsion—he *had*—to go through Samaria to fulfill his intention of addressing the Jewish-Samaritan divide.

As the disciples went off to find food, Jesus remained at Jacob's well, a well known to have been dug by the famous patriarch. That's where he encountered a Samaritan woman, a woman who had had her fill of ethnic strife and claims of ethnic superiority. After Jesus had asked her for a drink from the well, the woman asked, "How is it that you, a Jew, ask for a drink from me, a woman of Samaria?" John parenthetically explains the context of her question. "For Jews have no dealings with Samaritans" (John 4:9).

Her question was brazen, especially since in the first century she should have been timid and deferential in the presence of a man. One can easily hear her tone that indicated more of an accusation than a genuine inquiry. *Leave me alone, Jewish man. I certainly don't have to bow to your requests just because I'm a Samaritan.* I empathize with her attitude. Like me, the aftertaste of being made to feel inferior lingered with her. Unlike eleven-year-old me, however, the Samaritan woman had had enough and was ready for a confrontation.

Being denigrated based on one's race or ethnicity is one of the worst forms of injustice a person can suffer. The trauma results in a sensitivity that is so readily triggered that it may become a preoccupation that practically becomes part of one's identity. Ethnicity is an immutable human characteristic. Further, it is a neutral characteristic that carries no moral weight. Thus, to discriminate against someone on such a basis is the height of arbitrary and capricious judgment. More than that, such discrimination assaults another's very personhood and right to exist. As a result, we can become so preoccupied responding to the attack that defensiveness becomes our identity. Ultimately, the assault on our identity can be so successful that we don't know who we are absent the assaults and our reactions to them. Such a robbery is tragic indeed.

Perhaps that was roiling in the Samaritan woman's heart and mind as she encountered Jesus. Perhaps the mere sight of a Jewish man sitting on her people's well, seeming to make demands of her, was enough to trigger her past trauma. A clue about her feelings comes from the fact that her second question to Jesus fixed on ethnic tensions. In response to her accusation about Jewish self-superiority, Jesus pointed to his identity as the "gift of God" (John 4:10). His claim was just as brazen as her initial question, especially given the setting. A game of identity politics began as she immediately defended her ethnic heritage as a riposte to his audacious identity claim. "Are you greater than *our* father Jacob?" she asked. "He gave *us* the well and drank from it himself, as did his sons and his livestock" (v. 12, emphasis added).

Jesus' answer remarkably contrasts the combative way identity discussions typically happen, even today, when race becomes the reagent that turns a conversation into a conflict. If it were true that the Bible condones racism and ethnic superiority, we would expect Jesus to put the Samaritan woman in her place. Defying these expectations and defying the pattern we'd see today, Jesus directs her to focus on her spiritual identity by recognizing Jesus' true identity. "But whoever drinks of the water that I will give him will never be thirsty again. The water that I will give him will become in him a spring of water welling up to eternal life" (John 4:14). Jesus answered her ethnically charged question—"Are you greater than *our* father Jacob" who "gave *us* the well?"—with a yes. But his response didn't stem from ethnicity or race. He was the same ethnicity as Jacob. Nor was he claiming superiority as a Jew relative to a Samaritan. Rather, he claimed the authority to restore the image of God stamped on her because he is the incarnation of God. Through his identity, she would come to see the lasting value of her ethnic identity.

This is one of my favorite encounters in the Bible because it drips with authenticity. Jesus miraculously revealed that he knew the woman's ethnic struggles and moral past. She naturally acknowledged that he was a prophet. Now, a Hollywood-created exchange would have the woman instantly mesmerized, her issues resolved as music accompanied the setting sun. But in John's gospel, we read life's messy realism. A realistic account would depict someone whose life has been beset with ethnically driven mistreatment dealing with that mistreatment even after spiritual and emotional breakthroughs. The Bible records exactly that. "*Our* fathers worshiped on *this* mountain, but you say that in Jerusalem is the place where people ought to worship," the Samaritan woman continued (John 4:20, emphasis added). She referred to Mount Gerizim, the Samaritans' holiest site, as opposed to the Jews' holy site of the temple in Jerusalem. For her, the location of true worship was not a trivial matter. It was a question about the legitimacy of her ethnic identity. About two hundred years before, Jews had obliterated the Samaritans' temple on Mount Gerizim. The Samaritans retaliated by trying to deface the Jewish temple. Gerizim was in plain sight from Jacob's well where she and Jesus conversed. The scars of ethnic conflict and rejection were visible both figuratively and literally. One cannot help but picture how such an exchange might play out today, perhaps on a bench just in front of the "Wales Window" at 16th Street Baptist Church in Birmingham, Alabama, where four little girls were killed in a KKK bombing.

Jesus addressed her wounds in a surprising way. He pointed out that *neither* the Samaritan mountain *nor* the Jewish temple were ultimately important for our relationship with the divine (John 4:21). "But the hour is coming, and is now here," Jesus said, "when the true worshipers will worship the Father in spirit and truth, for the Father is seeking such people to worship him" (v. 23). We mustn't miss the sublime subtlety here. The woman staked her identity on her physiological father, Jacob, and the real estate he bequeathed. Jesus pointed her to her spiritual identity as a child of the transcendent Father and the restoration he offers. Her belonging comes from communion with him based on spirit and truth, not DNA and geography. "God is spirit, and those who worship him must worship in spirit and truth," Jesus said (v. 24). If that is not inclusive, it's hard to imagine what is.

F. W. Boreham's essay "Our Rubbish-Heaps" comes to my mind.[5] His point is that we tend to overcherish material and corporeal things regardless of our worldview. And yet the material world is constantly decaying into rubbish heaps. "Materialism, unmasked, appears as the religion of the rubbish-heap," Boreham wrote. Yet we cleave to material things as if they have lasting value on their own. Ethnicity is an important part of what it means to be human. For the strict materialist, however, ethnicity is only a material part of humanness and thus is as much a decaying part of our world as covered bridges. The secular rush to prioritize, even sacralize, race is a religion of the rubbish heap.

Boreham was quick to point out that for the religious ritualist, material worship is just as seductive and disappointing. "Ritualism stands in perilous relationship to the rubbish-heap," Boreham continued. After all, "The moth is in our fairest fabrics, and our holiest temples totter to their fall." On one occasion, Jesus predicted that the sacred temple of Jerusalem—the very temple the Samaritan woman pitted against Gerizim—would one day be destroyed.[6] For Boreham, hope placed even in deteriorating religious artifacts and places results in a deteriorating hope. "'Now abideth'—what?" he asked. "Altars? Vestments? Crosses? Creeds? Catechisms? Confessions?" The answer is in the famous passage from 1 Corinthians 13. "'Now abideth faith, hope, love these three; and the greatest of these is love.'"

This doesn't trivialize the material aspects of our existence. On the contrary, in the Christian faith, we will be resurrected with physical bodies and dwell in a physical world so glorified that it will be an amalgam of the corporeal and the ethereal. In other words, the transcendent aspects of reality sacralize the material aspects.

Jesus rose from the grave physically—to show us that eventually the law of deterioration would cease and rubbish heaps would be no more. Our ethnicities will not be washed away in the next life. The fleeting identity idols we have set up will be transformed into indelible aspects of our eternal identities. That is not a crumbling hope that depends on governmental policies or social justice. Rather, governmental policies and social justice can find true substance in eternal verities. Boreham had it right when he said, "It is well to set our affections on the things for which the rubbish-heap can have no terrors."

NEVER ENOUGH?

The film *Green Book* provides a contemporary illustration of how reliance on earthly identity leaves us wanting.[7] *Green Book* is based on the true story of two very different men. Dr. Donald Shirley is an African American world-class pianist who is about to start a concert tour of the Jim Crow era Deep South. It was hardly expected to be a safe journey. Enter Tony "Lip" Vallelonga, a streetwise, working-class Italian from the Bronx who knows how to handle himself in a tough spot. Dr. Shirley hires Tony not only to handle his travel itinerary but also to handle the racially based trouble that is sure to erupt.

After a predictably rough start, the two bond. Tony discovers that Dr. Shirley has never heard a song by African American legends Chubby Checker or Little Richard. Dr. Shirley grew up in fine-art circumstances, his virtuosity taking him around the world but shielding him from pop culture. Accordingly, Dr. Shirley struggles to identify with other African Americans whose workaday lives, music, and food are far different from his upbringing. Yet, because of his color, he's not truly welcomed among white folks either. Despite headlining concerts for mostly white audiences and being far more cosmopolitan, Dr. Shirley isn't allowed to eat with them in fancy dining rooms while Tony, his uncouth white driver, is.

On a rainy nighttime drive to another performance, Tony's talkativeness (hence the nickname Lip) ventures into the topic of identity. Tony, who struggles to make ends meet for his family, says that he's more in touch with black folks than Dr. Shirley is. After all, Tony knows their foods, he knows their music, and he shares their economic struggles. This strikes a nerve in Dr. Shirley. He has never felt at home with anyone, black or white. A lifetime of painfully living as an outsider boils to the surface as he shouts for Tony to stop the car.

He bursts out into the pouring rain, marching toward nowhere. Tony hurries after him, wondering what has upset his friend. Dr. Shirley spins to fill him in. "If I'm not white enough, if I'm not black enough, and I'm not man enough, then what am I?" he chokes out through rain-mixed tears.

This is the kind of complexity within which African Americans —especially Christians who wanted to rely on the church for hope—struggled for civil rights. It is likely still the case that this complexity persists today. This is the very complexity with which the Samaritan woman at Jacob's well lived. As a Samaritan, she wasn't Jewish enough. As a woman with a complicated marital history, she wasn't quite Samaritan enough. So what was she? The wounds of being caught in the middle came to identify her just as they came to identify Dr. Shirley.

FINDING OUR "ENOUGHS"

The Samaritan woman was on the verge of grasping the grand truth that ethnicity is important but is not ultimately defining. On another occasion, recorded in Luke 10, Jesus made this point with an expert in the Mosaic law who publicly challenged him. That man asked what he must do to have eternal life. Jesus said to love God and to love his neighbor as himself. The expert pressed a follow-up question, "And who is my neighbor?" (v. 29). Fascinatingly, Jesus answered with the parable of the good Samaritan, in which a priest and a Levite (both Jews of high religious stature) left an injured man to die on the side of a road for fear of being defiled. But a Samaritan came along and risked everything to help the man. Jesus made a Samaritan the protagonist and the true neighbor to induce a visceral reaction in his Jewish audience. He made the point—among many others—that godly love transcends ethnicity while also embracing it. In the same way, Jesus helped the Samaritan woman realize that her ethnically motivated mistreatment had robbed her of that which is most profound—her intrinsic value, regardless of ethnicity, before God.

Jesus' exchange with the Samaritan woman in John 4 ended with a disclosure that is quite rare for Jesus in terms of its bluntness.

After Jesus prophetically revealed her past, the woman at the well began to see that he might be the Messiah. She said, "I know that Messiah is coming (he who is called Christ). When he comes, he will tell us all things" (v. 25). To this point in John's gospel, whenever he was accosted by the religiously pious or self-assured, Jesus veiled his messianic identity in prophecies and parables. But to this Samaritan woman of little or no stature, he unveiled his identity plainly. "I who speak to you am he" (v. 26).

Just before that revelation, Jesus had seemed to engage in race-baiting. "Salvation is from the Jews," he said to her (John 4:22). In doing so, however, Jesus wasn't emphasizing ethnic superiority, but God's unmerited grace. God used the Jews, a lowly and unremarkable nation, to bring his message of love to the world. Ultimately, the embodiment of God's interaction with humanity is in the incarnation of God in Christ—Jesus the Jew from the marginal town of Nazareth. How transformative for the marginalized Samaritan woman to learn that the seemingly lowly are invited into God's family! Through his interaction with the woman at the well, Jesus tells us that the identity that bears the stamp of equality is not the identity borne of ethnicity, but the identity that bears the *imago Dei*.

Indeed, so transformative was this message of equality that the Samaritan woman ran from the well, leaving her water jug behind, so that she could urge her Samaritan village to personally encounter the Messiah. Perhaps it was the fire in her eyes or the glow of restoration that convinced her village. It certainly wasn't her communal prestige. But many from her village—a village that despised Jews—came to have a three-day encounter with Jesus and ultimately believed that he is the Savior of the world.

That reconciliation was nothing short of amazing. In today's terms, it would be as unlikely as Black Lives Matter protestors reconciling their differences and finding restorative friendships with Defend the Blue advocates all because an African American mother who lost her child to police violence pressed for the meeting.

An additional detail in the account demands our attention. As the Samaritan woman excitedly rushed off to her village, Jesus' Jewish disciples returned with food. As they did, "they marveled that he was talking with a woman, but no one said, 'What do you seek?' or, 'Why are you talking with her?'" (John 4:27). In other words, their ethnic prejudices led to indifference and possibly even disdain for the woman and her concerns. This wouldn't be the only time they would express such animosity toward Samaritans. In Luke 9:51–56 we read that an entire Samaritan village had rejected Jesus because he was Jewish. Incensed by the Samaritans' rejection, Jesus' disciples sought divine vengeance. "Lord, do you want us to tell fire to come down from heaven and consume them?" (v. 54). Jesus shocked them with a rebuke. Unlike his judgmental disciples, Jesus wanted to give the Samaritans every chance to repent before the ultimate judgment would come to the whole world.

Jesus' lessons eventually broke through the stubborn and sinful hearts and minds of his disciples. We read in Acts 8 that after Jesus' death, resurrection, and ascension to heaven, those same Jewish disciples, who once held nothing but contempt for Samaritans, now urged Samaritans to accept God's invitation for salvation. They not only preached but worked to help the Samaritan community. And the Samaritan community came to believe in Jesus as the one who infused their lives with meaning and value. This small detail in the book of Acts is breathtaking when we consider the depth of the disciples' transformation—from wanting to call down fire to consume the Samaritans to being consumed by a fiery love for them.

The Samaritans didn't have to be Jewish enough or Samaritan enough to merit the offer of eternal life. They only had to see enough that Jesus—and eventually the cross he bore as an infinite payment by an infinite God for a penalty we have all equally incurred—was the way to an everlasting peace with God and one another. And this started with a seemingly insignificant Samaritan woman who was so transformed by her spiritual reconciliation to God that she worked toward ethnic reconciliation among her community. That is the impact Jesus can have on every person he meets. He ennobles the lowly and dignifies the disdained. At the pizza shop, I was despised and rejected by a man with ethnic hate in his heart. Christ—who was despised and rejected by humanity—equally offers all ethnicities God's love.

THEORIES MEET *THEOS*

Some of our secular social theories contribute valuable insights to our conversations about racial inequities. These theories don't necessarily claim to offer solutions; they provide analyses based on historical and contemporary sociological data. And because that data has some flux, those theories need constant reevaluation, and like all theories, they need to be critiqued. One common critique is that they swing from one extreme to another. They either go too far in emphasizing a single factor that perpetuates all racial inequity, or not far enough in analyzing why humanity can't progress past our inequities. They don't account for the reality that human existence is a paradox of equally possessed *dignity* and equally possessed *depravity*—a paradox necessitating divine redemption. The gospel alone accounts for this paradox and provides a stable platform of transcendence on which our theories may find balance. The gospel provides a balanced corrective, limiting secular theories' overemphases while simultaneously liberating them from their limited scopes.

Accordingly, we shouldn't be surprised when we find some common ground between social theories and the Bible. We should view this common ground as an opportunity to explore the unique contribution the gospel makes in addressing racism.[8] For example, many social theorists acknowledge that "race" is a social construct that classifies people mainly by their outward physical characteristics. Yet scientifically speaking, genetic differences between people of different races are, in fact, *smaller* than those of people within the same race. Ethnicity, on the other hand, distinguishes people more broadly—somewhat on physical traits, but more prominently on the basis of cultural differences, beliefs, and behaviors. Although both race and ethnicity have been used to justify discrimination, race has made it possible for some to argue that certain people (regardless of their ethnicity) were physically and immutably inferior to others. From this logic flowed the justification for the enslavement of peoples and colonization of their lands. While the immorality of such thinking was obvious to many Westerners, those justifying slavery argued that it was no more or less immoral to enslave an African or take his land than to saddle a horse and fence off the land on which it had once run free.

The Bible agrees with the claim that race is a social construct. The Bible describes Middle Easterners, Asians, Africans, and Europeans, yet it doesn't employ race to divide humanity based on physical appearance. The Bible refers to different people groups— often along tribal, regional, and religious lines—but not primarily based on physical traits. Now, a moment's pause is in order. The Bible, long, long ago, *refused* to divide people along color lines. That this ancient, supposedly outdated document describes the world in ways we are only recently acknowledging through science should be a clue that there is something that signals its timeless and different ethic. The Bible does *not* commend making moral distinctions between people based on their physical appearances. Rather, in the Bible God judged and blessed different people groups' actions as expressions of their moral and religious beliefs. To paraphrase Dr. King's famous words, God makes judgments based on the content of people's character, not the color of their skin.

Further, modern social theories on race emphasize the bifurcation of society into the oppressed and their oppressors. While some have criticized this as myopic, the Christian faith also finds some agreement with this notion, calling us to be vigilant against oppression and to be mindful of how we might become oppressors. Anyone who reads the Bible cannot help but come away seeing God as committed to ending the oppressor-oppressed dichotomy. The Bible is replete with accounts of oppression, as well as numerous pleas by prophets and psalmists for God to break that oppression and eventually balance justice's scales.

The Christian message takes both of the key affirmations of social theories on race—that race is a social construct and society is composed of oppressors and oppressed—and tempers them. Ironically, these commonalities serve only to point out the deeper differences between our modern social theories and biblical ethics.

First, let's consider critical race theory (CRT), which acknowledges that race is a social construct that has been used to foster disempowerment. Kimberlé Crenshaw, like many CRT advocates, turns that disempowerment on its head by encouraging African Americans to embrace race as their primary, and thus empowering, identification:

We all can recognize the distinction between the claims "I am Black" and the claim "I am a person who happens to be Black. . . ." "I am Black" becomes not simply a statement of resistance but also a positive discourse of self-identification, intimately linked to celebratory statements like the Black nationalist "Black is beautiful." "I am a person who happens to be Black," on the other hand, achieves self-identification by straining for a certain universality (in effect, "I am first a person") and for a concomitant dismissal of the imposed category ("Black") as contingent, circumstantial, nondeterminant.[9]

Crenshaw expresses something important here that we mustn't dismiss. Identifying with one's race can be individually empowering because it allows a person to acknowledge the value of their ethnicity while simultaneously undermining the oppressor's original intent—to use racial labels to demean people—turning them instead into labels that dignify ethnic minorities. This seems especially worthwhile given that some ethnic minorities, most notably African Americans, historically have had no choice but to define themselves by their racial labels for a host of reasons. Racial labels have shaped their history and present-day living. To turn that label into a marker of dignity instead of derision is subversively empowering indeed.

But is this, in itself, a solution? Sadly, some continue down this path, moving from *significantly* identifying themselves by their race to *primarily* defining themselves this way. This infuses a social fiction with definitional dominion. That in turn risks transforming race from a mere social construct into a set of definitional knives by which we carve up a racialized society. Partitions of "they" and "we" are equally likely and perhaps perpetually embedded in this system.

How ironic that secular efforts to transform a social construction meant to subjugate certain people through division can become the very means that further perpetuate the racial divisions those efforts sought to eliminate.

The gospel provides the needed balance. It values our ethnicities and even our unique ethnic identities—without endowing them with the definitional power that risks dividing us. God blesses us with ethnicity as an *expression* of who we are while endowing us with his image as a *definition* of what we are. Social and spiritual unity, therefore, doesn't have to entail sacrificing ethnic diversity. Jesus' conversation with the Samaritan woman expressed the proper balance. He didn't ignore that she was a Samaritan or that he was a Jew. To put it in contemporary terms, Jesus wasn't "color-blind." When someone asserts that they are "color-blind" and says, "I don't see race; I just see a person," they may mean well. But statements like these can also have ill effects, ignoring or minimizing the unique expression of identity that God has given a person of another ethnicity. Our ethnicities shape our thinking, our sensitivities, our perspectives, and even our cuisines. Telling a black person, "I don't see color," is tantamount to saying, "I don't really see you." Jesus wasn't color-blind. He saw the woman's Samaritan-ness. Yet in acknowledging who she was, he did not *reduce* her to her genetic code or socially constructed situation. Rather, she was *by definition* God's image-bearer and *by expression* a Samaritan. She bore the image that suffused her ethnicity with permanent value beyond her circumstances. God's image defined her general humanness; her ethnicity expressed her particular humanness.

Before meeting Jesus, this woman saw the world through ethnic definitions that divided the superior from the inferior. And her cynicism and bitterness almost blinded her to the truth about the value of the ethnically other (a Jewish man) and even her own value apart from the prejudice she had endured. Jesus acknowledged the injustices she had experienced while pointing her to a better path on which God-defined souls can find redemption.

Another point of contrast between secular theories and the gospel is how they explain the cause of racism. Secular theories can explain the symptoms of our ailment but not the underlying cause. To be fair, many of these theories may not even attempt to do more than analyze social phenomena. They will acknowledge our innate desire to grab and preserve power but stop there, not addressing why we seek this power. But the gospel goes deeper, diagnosing the root cause. The apostle Paul described our human penchant for suppressing truths and embracing falsehoods to elevate ourselves above God. We, by our "unrighteousness suppress the truth" (Rom. 1:18). As a result, we have become "inventors of evil" and "ruthless" (Rom. 1:28, 30–31). And history has proven Paul right. For centuries we have suppressed the truth about human equality and invented a falsehood about race to justify our ruthless evil. But the cause of that evil is deeper still. Because we want to be gods ourselves, we have suppressed the truth that we are made for communion with God. This leads us to invent the lie that God imposes restrictions on us to oppress our self-realization. It's little wonder, then, that in aggrandizing ourselves above humanity's Creator we end up abasing his creation to further exalt ourselves. Truth's suppression has led to ethnic oppression.

Secular theories may describe the branches of oppression's tree while the gospel exposes the root that feeds the tree. Jesus challenged his hearers and his followers—and us today—to consider the fact that sin will lead people to skirt laws in exploitative ways. We have laws aimed at ending discrimination, hate, and oppression.

Yet discrimination, hate, and oppression persist. Perhaps we simply need *more* of such laws to shape society. Or harsher consequences for those who break these laws.

But would that alone be a solution? When the rule of nature and the rule of law collide, the rule of nature usually wins. Our tax codes, with their regulations, subparts, and exemptions, are bloated. Our health care laws swell to similar bulk. There's a reason the United States Congress needed to enact the Civil Rights Act. There's a reason for the UN Charter on Human Rights. These laws and charters are not candelabras of the better angels of our natures but corks on the evil fizzing within us all.

The gospel singularly addresses the paradoxes of human morality. We exercise morality when we abide by laws, but we demonstrate our depravity by needing laws to abide by. We are beset by a sinful condition (Jer. 17:9; Matt. 15:19), yet we bear the divine image (Gen. 1:26–27). Blaise Pascal summed up the human paradox so well: "What a chimera then is man! What a novelty! What a monster, what a chaos, what a contradiction, what a prodigy! Judge of all things, imbecile worm of the earth; depositary of truth, a sink of uncertainty and error; the pride and refuse of the universe!"[10]

But God offers freedom from this wretched paradox. The redemptions of the human heart, the human mind, and to some degree even human laws and institutions, begin at the cross. The broader ethic of justice subsumes racial justice, after all. And at the cross, transcendent justice was meted out because human sin was punished and paid for. Mercy and forgiveness were dispensed to us because Jesus willingly paid our debt as our representative. In our current cultural moment, we rightly shout for justice but whisper about forgiveness. Yet reconciliation happens only when justice (getting what we deserve) and forgiveness (getting what we don't deserve) are simultaneously extended. The work we have yet to do on our laws, policies, and relationships to pursue ethnic justice must start from that gospel base. The cross resolves the nested paradoxes of human depravity and nobility and ultimate justice and forgiveness.

In Jesus' day, the ethnic dividing lines were just as sharp as ours today. Yet Paul, once so proud of being a Jew and *not* a Gentile, pointed to the person of Christ and his cross as the means for vertical peace with God that, when lived out, can lead to horizontal reconciliation with one another. "For he himself is our peace, who has made us both one and has broken down in his flesh the dividing wall of hostility" (Eph. 2:14). Paul taught that through Christ, in our position before God, we are "one new man"—meaning unified. The unifying "what" of humanity allows us to value our diverse "whos" without hostility. Theories alone have no such power without the *Theos*.

THE GOSPEL IN ACTION

Spiritual realities lay behind some of our most profound leaps forward in racial justice. The long-fought struggle to abolish the British slave trade comes to mind. William Wilberforce, the British parliamentarian, spearheaded the effort along with freed slaves and fellow Britons. Wilberforce's conversion to Christianity, ironically enough, almost caused him to retreat from public service for private ministry. But William Pitt, Wilberforce's friend and then prime minister of Great Britain, urged Wilberforce to use his newfound Christian convictions to serve the greater good through political means. John Newton, the former captain of a slave ship and writer of the world-famous hymn "Amazing Grace," urged Wilberforce to pursue his God-given calling into politics to effectuate change in Britain. With an invigorated faith in Christ, Wilberforce set out to accomplish his "two great aims"—the reformation of manners (meaning the revival of morality in Britain) and the abolition of the slave trade. Eventually Wilberforce opposed the institution of slavery altogether. Wilberforce recognized that to stamp out the evil of slavery, Britain's slumbering sense of transcendent morality would have to be roused. For that reawakening, Wilberforce and his friends of the Clapham sect appealed to the gospel message.

The famous image that seared itself onto British retinas and branded itself on British hearts was that of an African slave kneeling, asking the question, "Am I not a man and a brother?" An African slave's question elicited a "yes" from the white Britons because they were influenced by the olive-skinned gospel that declares all humans to be the bearers of God's very image. There is something poetic in the fact that this man-made image reminded those with political and social power of the divine image stamped on us all. Seeds planted by John Wesley's evangelism and social reform influenced many who would enter Parliament, including Wilberforce.[11] This is no small example of how gospel-inspired impulses work in symbiosis with social reform. Changed hearts led to changed morality, which led to changed legislation. True, it took decades to accomplish. But it likely never would have been accomplished were it not for the message of equality so profoundly uttered and demonstrated by the olive-skinned, brown-eyed, and black-haired Jesus.

Yet scholars like Steven Pinker want to credit social and moral advancement solely to a romanticized and secularized account of the Enlightenment. Pinker claims, "If there's anything the

Enlightenment thinkers had in common it was an insistence that we energetically apply the standard of reason to understanding our world and not fall back on generators of delusion like faith, dogma, revelation, authority, charisma, mysticism, divination, visions, gut feelings, or the hermeneutic parsing of sacred texts. It was reason that led most of the Enlightenment thinkers to repudiate the belief in an anthropomorphic God who took an interest in human affairs."[12] Writing as if Wilberforce and the successful Christian abolitionist movement had never existed, Pinker adds, "The Enlightenment is sometimes called the humanitarian revolution because it led to the abolition of barbaric practices that had been commonplace across civilizations for millennia. If the abolition of slavery and cruel punishment is not progress, nothing is."[13]

The glaring errors coming from such a brilliant man are legion. First, Pinker's secularized idealization of the Enlightenment omits influential Christian thinkers of that time. John Locke springs to mind as but one example. Second, it is undeniable that even the secular Enlightenment thinkers built their ideas on the foundations of Christian morality. Jens Zimmermann puts it well: "So-called Enlightenment values, such as social welfare and human rights, with foundational conceptions of human dignity, freedom, agency, rationality and personhood, all go back to Christian roots."[14]

Perhaps the biggest problem is philosophical. Pinker credits the human capacity for sympathy (coupled with reason) for humanitarian advances. So smitten with human nature is Pinker that he actually declares, "Given that we are equipped with the capacity to sympathize with others, nothing can prevent the circle of sympathy from expanding from the family and tribe to embrace all of humankind."[15] But a moment's reflection reveals that something can indeed prevent the circle of sympathy from expanding: the human capacity for antipathy. Another atheist, John Gray, would point out that we are actually more given to act with antipathy toward others than sympathy. As for the Enlightenment's supposed achievement of abolishing slavery, the fact is that some thinkers of the day were full-blown racists. David Hume dismissed the poetic genius of Jamaican-born Francis Williams as "one negro" who was likely "admired for very slender accomplishments, like a parrot who speaks a few words plainly."[16] Gray points out that some prominent Enlightenment thinkers advocated rationally applied violence. "Along with liberal humanists everywhere, [Pinker] regards the core of the Enlightenment as a commitment to rationality. The fact that prominent Enlightenment figures have favored violence as an instrument of social transformation is—to put it mildly—inconvenient."[17]

Pinker, like so many of us, assumes that as we swim in the stream of time and technological progress, our moral sensibilities grow stronger and things get better. To some extent that's true, of course. But when we pause to consider the fact that race-based chattel slavery became an international trade in contravention of biblical principles meant to abolish slavery and minimize debt servitude, we ought to be struck by the chronological irony. We claim that the Bible is an outmoded document unsuited to an enlightened age, yet the barbarism of slavery reached its institutional peak in the so-called Enlightenment and persists in the form of sex trafficking even today.

We ignore the gospel's influence on our past victories over the hell of prejudice at our peril. We fail to see the conflict between the philosophies of Pinker's optimistic call for "Enlightenment Now" and many social theorists' views that the West is terminally racist. Yet both are essentially secular humanist philosophies. Pinker would have us believe that the better angels of our nature (the title of one of his books) will continue to lead to ever-increasing flourishing.[18] Yet others claim that racism, conscious and unconscious, is omnipresent and impossible to stamp out. Surprisingly, the gospel message partially affirms insights from *both* views by synthesizing them with a solution. It tells us that human sin is so heinous that Jesus had to die on the cross to atone for it, yet his willingness to pay for our sin demonstrates the magnitude of God's value for humanity.

Marcello Pera, an atheist philosopher and politician, powerfully stated that so-called Enlightenment values owe their very existence to the gospel. Referring to the New Testament, Pera writes, "Does not this old fashioned booklet teach that men are the sons of God, created in his image, and therefore free, equal, and united by the same destiny? True, it took a long time and many troubles and tragedies to understand this message. But that means that the Enlightenment was late, not that it was new."[19]

GO BACK TO WHERE YOU CAME FROM

Allow me to close this discussion of Christianity and race by juxtaposing my "camel jockey" experience with what occurred to me as I neared my conversion to Christ. Quite a few obstacles impeded my investigation. First, I was a Muslim, and becoming a Christian would be a jarring shift in my religious identity, with social ripple effects. Second, though not as dire but still important, was my ethnic identity. I became a Christian in 2000, but in the months before that, my spiritual trek hit a roadblock.

In 1999 the so-called Y2K bug consumed social discourse. Everyone feared that computer systems that ran banking, utilities, schools, medical records, and everything in between that stored dates as "99" instead of "1999" would suddenly act as if it were 1900 instead of 2000 on January 1. People were planning for an apocalypse, and Christians were speaking especially about the end-times. Loud evangelical voices—even though they may have been the minority—were analyzing world events leading up to January 2000 and trying to pin the tail on the Antichrist. Because of the raging Middle East Conflict, some were focusing on the Arab-Israeli conflict. And with those discussions so ethnically focused, I couldn't help but wonder if Christianity wasn't really about God's love for the world as much as it was about God's love for particular people based on their ethnicity. And my ethnicity, as an Arab, was not on the favored list.

In those months, however, I pressed on with my spiritual search. Something drew me back to the passage of the Bible that got me thinking critically about matters of faith in the first place. Years before, I was reading the Bible to find flaws with it, to show Christians that the Bible couldn't be trusted. I had been asking Christians the question, "Why are you a Christian?" to which most responded, "I was raised that way." In other words, *tradition.* I would challenge them, asking how they could trust their soul's destiny to a worldview that they hadn't really thought through. But then I read the words of John the Baptist, which confronted the assumptions of those who were coming to him for baptism. "Who warned you to flee from the wrath to come?" John asked them, referring to the judgment coming to them due to their sins. "Bear fruits in keeping with repentance. *And do not begin to say to yourselves, 'We have Abraham as our father.' For I tell you, God is able from these stones to raise up children for Abraham*" (Luke 3:7–8, emphasis added). He made clear to his followers that tradition by itself does not save a person's soul. Truth does.

Those words struck me because I had been telling Christians

that their blind reliance on tradition was shortsighted and wrong-headed. And now I had found that John the Baptist was confronting me with my own argument. I had failed to realize that the underlying reason I was a Muslim was tradition. Sure, I had found arguments to support my beliefs, but the undercurrent to it all was tradition. Those two verses of the Bible set my mind on a path of seeking truth over tradition.

Back in 1999 another profound truth bubbled from those verses as the ethnic stumbling blocks popped up on the road toward faith in Christ. John the Baptist wasn't just challenging his followers' assumptions about spiritual traditions—he was challenging their ethnic pride. Yes, God had made a covenant with Abraham to bless his descendants the Israelites. Yet that covenant wasn't based on ethnic superiority or racial partiality. Being a Jew couldn't benefit the unrepentant heart. God could replace every single person listening to John with a person birthed out of stone. They didn't have to share Abraham's DNA to be considered Abraham's children—just his faith in the God of redemption. This meant that Jews, Arabs, Europeans, Africans, Asians, Australians, and everyone in between were invited into the family of God. Ethnicity was neither a VIP pass nor a barrier to God's embrace.

And yet our sublimely different ethnicities will persist into heaven. Heaven is not a gray sea diluted of color. The Bible describes the celestial city established at history's consummation as an eternal community of unity amid diversity. "And the city has no need of sun or moon to shine on it, for the glory of God gives it light, and its lamp is the Lamb. By its light will the *nations* walk, and the kings of the earth will bring their glory into it, and its gates will never be shut by day—and there will be no night there. They will bring into it the glory and the honor of the *nations*" (Rev. 21:23–26, emphasis added). Heaven will be filled with people of every color, much like a mosaic. The nations, with their wonderful diversities, will bring their temporal glories before God and submit them to his eternal glory. The ethnic diversity of the nations will persist even as the diverse nations bask in God's single glory.

Two stanzas from John Greenleaf Whittier's "Hymn" express this beautifully:

> When from each temple of the free,
> A nation's song ascends to Heaven,
> Most Holy Father! Unto Thee
> May not our humble prayer be given?
>
> Thy children all, though hue and form
> Are varied in Thine own good will,
> With Thy own holy breathings warm,
> And fashioned in Thine image still.[20]

There will be unity in diversity in heaven. We will offer our distinct colors, aromas, and spices to the master chef, who will offer to us one eternal banquet. We are all invited to go back to where we came from.

God's invitation expresses nothing like the contempt that man at the pizza shop had for me those years ago. He wanted me expelled from his world, telling me to go back to where I came from. In the gospel message, godly love inverts the hatred of such a statement. As I saw the credibility of the Christian faith, I uncovered God's call for me to return to him, to go back to the one from whom I came, the one for whom my Arab soul was made, the one for whom all souls were made.

PART 2

NOT JUST FOR MEN

CHAPTER 6

CHALLENGING THE INTERPRETATIONS OF THE TEXTS THAT CHALLENGE US

A GALVANIZED SEARCH

My first daughter's birth was pivotal for me in many ways. More accurately, that "pivot" likely started at the ultrasound appointment when my wife and I learned that the person living in her womb was a girl. The excitement at the thought of raising a girl mingled with anxiety borne of my unfamiliarity of living in a home with a little girl. I only have brothers in my family and grew up surrounded by uncles and male cousins. There were no "little girls" in our family.

As in some other cultures, Middle Easterners place a premium on having sons, especially as the firstborn. My firstborn happened to be a boy. But this cultural premium on male children goes beyond the first and extends to all births. Yes, little girls are cherished, but when Middle Eastern couples discover they are pregnant, most people (men and women alike) are likely to wish them the birth of a happy, healthy male child.

This always puzzled me as a child and again as a young man. Shouldn't we wish for just as many girls as boys? How else would we propagate humanity? Perhaps the answer would have been, "Of course, but let other people have the girls. For you, I hope for a boy." There's a strange kind of NIMBY ("not in my backyard") mentality there, similar to how people know that we need prisons, sanitation facilities, and factories, so long as they are near someone else's home. This mentality extends beyond Middle Eastern cultures. African, Asian, and Mediterranean cultures of Europe also have some of these same prejudices. I can't help but think of the wedding scene at the beginning of *The Godfather* where Luca Brasi congratulates Don Corleone on his daughter's new marriage by saying, "May their first child be a masculine child." The implication, if not the outright declaration, is that women are less valued than men.

At the same time, I grew up being taught to honor my mother and grandmother with the highest honors possible. When they spoke, I was to listen. So I was surrounded by mixed messages, and I suspect the same is true for many of us, regardless of which culture dominated our upbringings. In Western society, a woman's right to vote was only relatively recently recognized, and it is only in the past several decades that women's career successes have been celebrated. Whereas some cultures send mixed messages by valuing male children over females while honoring their mothers, Western cultures send a mixed message by championing women's rights while at the same time sexualizing and objectifying them. Misogyny is as old as history. It has a passport with many stamps.

Unsurprisingly, religion has been blamed for misogyny's inception and persistence. The mixed messages I received from both of my cultures (Middle Eastern and Western) influenced how I approached religious texts. Whether it was the Qur'an I studied growing up, the Bible I study today, or the Vedas and Bhagavad Gita I explored along the way, I can understand why many see these texts as sanctifying misogynist tendencies.

I became a Christian six years before my first daughter's birth. And I became a Christian only after scrutinizing the Bible and other religions (and atheism) for nine years before that. During those fifteen years, I wrestled with various religious texts that seemed to enlist God's imprimatur on male dominance. The Bible was no exception. Given the mingled nature of my understanding about male-female dynamics, I was both unsurprised and troubled by what I was reading in some religious texts and the interpretations given them by religious scholars. Given my own affinity for examining propositional truth claims—whether factual or philosophical—the main focus of my spiritual exploration was on whether any of those texts offered verifiable and falsifiable claims. While my empirical examination yielded answers, the moral facets of religious belief, including (and especially) male-female dynamics, remained for me. They lingered patiently in the background of my exploration, waiting for my attention.

I came to faith largely because the evidence for Christianity's chief miracle—Jesus' bodily resurrection—is strong despite the miracle's antiquity. Yet many others today won't even consider that historical evidence. Why? Because they first see evidence of moral deficiencies, particularly in the Bible's denigration of women. In some regards, my own investigative path looks like a photo negative of the path others take today. Some (like me) tackle factual claims to arrive at moral truths. Others (like many today) use morality to determine whether factual claims are even worth examining in the first place. Bible scholar James Hurley recounts this doubt a friend expressed to him: "It's one thing to believe that a man rose from the dead or that he could change water to wine. Those things were long ago and are so foreign to me that I can accept them. It is a lot harder to accept that my wife needs to go around veiled and meekly to accept any crazy thing which I decide. It almost seems that she is put down by the Bible."[1]

Hurley's friend could accept the miracle stories because they happened so long ago and were so foreign to his experience today, yet he couldn't accept the Bible's statements about women's and men's roles. Weren't those statements uttered just as long ago as the miracles happened? Weren't they uttered in a faraway, foreign place and time with a different context? So why would physical and temporal distance make miracles more acceptable while what the Bible says about men and women is inexcusable—regardless of time and space? Perhaps what he's saying is that we can be morally justified in accepting the miracles on faith, but given our modern enlightenment, we simply cannot accept what the Bible has to say about gender. If we pay attention, however, this criticism contains its own response. This man acknowledged that the miracle claims had to be understood *in their contexts*. I would argue similarly for what the Bible says about men and women—it should be understood that way too. And what may surprise us is how understanding this historical context reveals Christianity's contemporary applications.

My own exploration of the Christian message's truth yielded an implied answer to any quandary I had about women in the Bible. If the evidence established the Bible's chief miracle claims, then there must be a God who cares deeply about humanity's plight. And if there is proof of that, then my anxieties over the Bible's so-called troubling texts were more likely due to my own misunderstandings. The strong light of the empirical evidence of biblical accounts provided hope that my beclouded interpretations would dissipate. Getting married and having two girls of my own galvanized that hope and has, in fact, led to a clearer understanding. I'm convinced that the Bible pulses with affirmations of women's equality and dignity. And so I concur with Hurley's responsive thought to his friend's critique. "I'm glad that the husband whom I have quoted did not really understand what the Bible says about the relation of husbands to wives."[2]

BROADENING OUR FOCUS, SHARPENING OUR VISION

It should be obvious by now, given my focus on ferreting out which worldview would offer me empirically verifiable truth, that I was not (nor am today) a postmodernist. However, if postmodernism bequeathed any gift to the world, it is the understanding that we all approach particular texts with personal baggage, whether cultural, familial, or experiential. We are not the blank slates of objectivity we fancy ourselves to be. This realization can help us go about the task of removing blind spots that endanger a proper interpretation of a text, including a text like the Bible. Rather than merely seeing their faulty reading of the Bible as a blind spot, when it comes to what the Bible says about women, many today believe themselves already to be fully sighted. Just google phrases like "the Bible and women" or "women in the Old Testament," and you will no doubt find, shall we say, interesting reading. Critics believe that spotlighting the Bible's teaching on women exposes a deity Richard Dawkins calls the "misogynistic" God of the Old and New Testaments.[3] Ironically, critics like Dawkins lament that religious fundamentalists read their sacred texts woodenly and without critical examination of their methods. Yet those very critics frequently approach the Bible with the same hermeneutic they lament. In Dawkins's case, his fundamentalist and wooden reading of the Bible didn't spawn an extremist, but a straw man.

An illustration will spotlight the flaw in Dawkins's criticism. One night an aficionado of murder movies espies something alarming at his neighbor's house and immediately calls 911. A man wildly hacks at his neighbors' door with an ax. With every swing, the man screams, "I'm coming for you!" Finally destroying the door, the man eagerly rushes in and seconds later drags the unsuspecting and distraught neighbors out of the house. The 911 caller is convinced that he is witnessing a murder in progress, only to be puzzled when the man bizarrely douses the neighbors with water. What the 911 caller failed to take into consideration in this absurdly myopic illustration is that had he not been so fixated on interpreting the events within his obsession of horror movies, he might have seen that the house was on fire and the supposed maniac was really saving his neighbors' lives, not taking them.

Something similar happens with some interpretations of the Bible. We come to the text with a particular fixation on certain details and we miss the fire that caused this specific text to be written in the first place. Perhaps our narrow views come from bad examples of those who call themselves Christians, or perhaps they are shaped by a traumatic event. We view the Bible through the lenses of such experiences rather than the broader context. Perhaps what we are witnessing in the God of the Bible's character is not a twisted maniac terrorizing people in their homes, but a public servant seeking to rescue those in danger.

The birth of my first daughter broadened my vision about women's experiences and how the Bible has been misused to taint those experiences. It also sharpened my vision to focus on that which I had only passingly glanced at in my spiritual journey—the biblical texts about women and how they depict a God who has heard their cries, drawn them to Christ, and blessed them with the opportunity to fuel the surge of Christianity.

ON THE EVE OF EQUALITY

Where the Bible gets on the wrong foot, critics argue, is right at the very beginning; as a matter of fact, it is "in *the* beginning." We learn of Eve's particular creation in Genesis 2:21–22, and right away two thoughts grip us: Eve is a derivative of Adam, and her role in life is to be his inferior "helpmate." God created her not as an equal partner for Adam, but as something like his Stepford wife. If Eve or any other women wanted to leave their oppressive servant roles, God's law would immediately halt them by preventing them from divorcing their husbands. If a woman thought she might be able to live without a man in this hellish world, she should think again: God commanded that only male children would gain an inheritance. Women would be stuck as *de jure* and *de facto* slaves in their households, forced to love one man who was free to love as many women as he wanted. A husband provided four walls and a roof, yes, but those four walls would form a cell for the second-class, derivative slave human called "woman."

There can be no doubt that some treatment of women by Christians has inculcated this interpretation of the Bible. It is easy to reason that if a biblically literate Christian says that their unimpeachable interpretation of the Bible means a woman's subjugation, then that interpretation must be correct. The problem in our minds, then, is not with the interpreter, but with the text itself. But, as we will see, such judgments are fraught with false assumptions.

If our misunderstandings take root at the Bible's beginning, then so might the needed clarifications. Eve's creation in Genesis 2, while maligned as depicting Eve as merely derivative of Adam, being formed from his rib, actually speaks to the equal nature the original couple were meant to have. Adam lovingly calls Eve "bone of my bones and flesh of my flesh" (v. 23), and this intimate relationship is a model for all marital relationships where men and women come together and become "one flesh," which is to say, unified in mind, body, and spirit. This is not a sign of inferiority, but an indication of Eve's equality. She wasn't taken from Adam's feet, which might be a sign of inferiority as it is in the early Vedic Brahma creation myth that establishes the caste system. Nor was she taken from his head, which may have been seen as a sign of superiority. Rather, she was created from Adam's side. The apostle Paul reminded any man who saw in Eve's creation anything that might justify male preeminence to remain humble. "For as woman was made from man, so man is now born of woman. And all things are from God" (1 Cor. 11:12).

The charge of "derivative" also loses sight of what is affirmed of women in Genesis 1 and 2 before we even read of Eve's creation. Genesis 1 is a summary statement of creation that doesn't so much give us precise details as it describes to us who God is, what creation is, and who we are. In Genesis 1:27 we get the foundational message about humanity that will be the basic background understanding of everything we read about women in the Bible: "So God created mankind in his own image, in the image of God he created them; male and female he created them" (NIV). This statement, which at the beginning of Scripture sets the tone for the rest of Scripture, declares that both men and women are created in God's image. There is no weaker side of God that created a weaker sex; there is no "lesser" creation in women than in men. Both are created in the image of God. This basic truth undergirds every verse in the Bible about women. It is the broth that the biblical stew is simmered in.

The charge that the Bible suggests Eve's inferiority by labeling her Adam's "helpmate" (*ezer* in Hebrew) is a spice foreign to the biblical recipe. In the context, Eve's status as a helpmate is as far from a label of inferiority as one can find. Adam needs Eve precisely because he was incomplete without her. When the Bible says that Eve was created for the sake of man, that is not for the sake of man's pleasure or dominion, but rather to address his vulnerabilities and loneliness. In the creation of the first people, we witness parallel vulnerabilities. Where men might be considered physically stronger than women (as we will see in the New Testament), women might be considered relationally more adept than men. This is admittedly speculative, but perhaps a reason that Eve is created from Adam's rib is that ribs protect one's heart. Nevertheless, a man needing a woman for emotional fulfillment is an ancient, time-tested rebuttal to the tired idea that a "macho" man is one of stoic insensitivity and invulnerability. The Bible, properly understood, confronts the so-called toxic masculinity it is often blamed for.

Eve's label of "helpmate" is linked to the purpose for which she and Adam are called as a couple. The Bible describes the first marriage—performed by God himself—as one of unity in diversity undergirded by equality. "Therefore a man shall leave his father and his mother and hold fast to his wife, and they shall become *one flesh*" (Gen. 2:24, emphasis added). The Hebrew word translated "one flesh" reveals a deep beauty about why men and women are created together. That word, in Hebrew, is *echad*. It can mean one in a numerical sense, but its more common meaning is one as in *unified*. The Bible refers to a single cluster of grapes, for example, as an *echad* cluster of grapes (Num. 13:23).

The depth of the term *echad* and what it means for Adam and Eve's positions is highlighted in the famous Hebrew Shema, found in Deuteronomy 6:4. The Shema is a creed-like phrase by which the nation of Israel identified itself as distinct from the pagans around them: "Hear, O Israel: The LORD our God, the LORD is one." The word for "one" here is *echad*, which again usually signifies unity rather than numerical singleness. This phrase gives us a hint of the divine Trinity. In the Christian faith, God exists as one being with three distinct coeternal, coexistent persons. The Father is God, the Son is God, and the Holy Spirit is God. Each is a distinct person in that each is a distinct consciousness, yet they all share the same and singular nature of being God.[4] Each person of the Trinity, though distinct in their personhood, is eternally coequal. More simply put, God himself exists as a unified diversity. In fact, in the Shema, the word "God" is actually plural, such that the phrase literally states, "Here, O Israel: The LORD our *Gods* [plural], the LORD is *unified*." Through their marriage, Adam and Eve were equally empowered with the ability to be a unified diversity. They were one flesh, but they retained their individual personhood and equality. They—and by extension every woman and man born since—are invited to reflect something of God's nature.

Eve, however, in being labeled a "helpmate" (*ezer*) was given the particular honor of sharing that appellation with God himself. God is the one who "helps" Israel (Ps. 89:19). One of Moses' sons received a name derived from this word, Eliezer, meaning "The God of my father was my help, and delivered me from the sword of Pharaoh" (Ex. 18:4). Yes, the God who mightily rescued Israel from slavery under the oppressive Egyptian regime was Israel's helpmate in that moment. The word itself, *ezer*, is actually derived from two other words meaning "strength" and "to rescue." The psalmist cried out to this God, "I am poor and needy; come quickly to me, O God. You are my help and my deliverer; LORD, do not delay" (Ps. 70:5 NIV). This is a helpfulness derived from strength rather than subordination. Interestingly, Adam already had a helper in God, who was superior to him, and a helper in animals, which were inferior to him. Yet God created Eve, a helper "suitable" for Adam, which is to say an equal counterpart.[5]

I heard some valuable insights about the Bible's distinctiveness from philosopher and theologian William Lane Craig. Like the Bible, other ancient Near Eastern religions offer accounts of creation, usually with gods subduing the elements and battling to bring order out of chaos. These religions describe humanity's creation in general but don't focus on women at all. Craig observed, "Ancient Mesopotamian myths about human creation usually refer to humanity's creation in terms of slave labor for the gods. And they never (so far as I could tell) mention the creation of women (or they don't have any excursus on the creation of women). The fact that the Bible does shows: (1) it doesn't really borrow from other myths; and (2) it is unique in its focus on women and equality.

This may seem like a small semantic point, but it simply cannot be missed."[6] Perhaps another observation will drive the point home. Diane Langberg notes that while God commands Adam and Eve (as humanity's federal representatives) to rule over and subdue the earth, "the man is not told to rule over the woman; neither is the woman to rule over the man. They are to rule together, in a duet, over all else God created."[7]

Modern critics would charge that Eve was perhaps the Bible's original scapegoat in that she is blamed for seductively leading a good man astray to eat forbidden fruit, which ultimately caused humanity to be cast out of Eden. Interestingly, God didn't immediately confront Eve after she and Adam ate the fruit God specifically prohibited. He confronted Adam. "Have you eaten of the tree of which I commanded you not to eat?" God asked him (Gen. 3:11). Why did God confront Adam and not Eve? Perhaps the answer is that Adam was her representative. Perhaps it was because while Eve was deceived by the serpent, the most cunning of all creatures, Adam allowed himself to be deceived by another human. It is possible that God was revealing to Adam the weaker state of his will. We get a glimpse of this in Adam's response to God's question: "The woman whom *you gave* to be with me, she gave me fruit of the tree, and I ate" (Gen. 3:12). Adam blamed not only Eve for his choice but God for bringing Eve into the picture.

Remarkably, an interpretive tradition that places all blame on Eve, taking Adam's side as a victim, has persisted despite the text's clarity. I will say more on this in a moment. Suffice it to say for now that the willingness of some learned men to grossly misinterpret this account to lay more blame at Eve's feet and absolve Adam as the helpless victim speaks more about their sexist hearts than it does about the morality of the biblical text.

A STUDY IN CONTRASTS: MARRIAGE AND SEX IN THE BIBLE COMPARED TO ANCIENT NEAR EASTERN RELIGIONS

Another thorny aspect of the biblical text is the numerous marriage laws. Don't biblical marriage laws create a state of gender inequality? Some argue that the Old Testament demands a woman had to stay committed and servile if she found herself unlucky enough to be married to an Israelite man. And even if she could get away, she would have no means of supporting herself, for her husband would get everything in the divorce, and women at that time received no inheritance from their fathers. We see examples today of women who have been manipulated into staying in dangerous situations by using their own heartfelt faith and the threat of financial ruin against them. As it turns out once again, however, the case against the Bible is not as simple as it has been made out to be.

Contrasting biblical marriage with those of the nearby cultures of Assyria and Babylon can give us some perspective. Babylon was, compared to Assyria, a bit more lenient in these areas. A husband could divorce a wife very easily and seemingly on a whim, but a wife could also divorce, though she had to take him to a court of law to do so. And taking him to court brought serious risks for her. If her suit was legitimate, he would have to return her dowry to her, but other than that he faced no penalties. But if the suit was deemed illegitimate, the wife would be drowned. If the husband brought a successful suit against his wife, penalties following a divorce ranged from financial destitution to possible enslavement.[8] Ultimately, "Babylonian women were legally subordinate to their fathers and to their husbands."[9] Assyrian culture, on the other hand, did not provide any recourse—legal or otherwise—for women to divorce their husbands. Even a legitimate widow had a difficult life in Assyria. Women were considered to be the property of their fathers or husbands. This is why adultery was treated as a form of property damage in the ancient Assyrian law codes. Men could not legally be considered adulterers; women caught in adultery, however, were subject to a range of punishments "from verbal rebuke to disfigurement to dismemberment to execution." As Hurley succinctly states, "It is always the husband who is the offended party."[10] This aspect is similar to Babylonian/Mesopotamian laws that, while carrying heavy sentences for people caught in adultery, define sex outside of marriage as adultery only if the woman is married (or in one instance, if the woman is the virgin slave of another man). This meant married men could freely seek prostitutes, which was considered a fundamental right due to the Gilgamesh Epic's depiction of Enkidu with a prostitute.[11] Despite the differences in the Babylonian and Assyrian legal codes' harshness, they shared the underlying belief that women were property belonging to men.

Since Israelite culture belongs to roughly the same geographic and cultural milieu as these cultures, we would expect to see similarities to the Babylonians and Assyrians. And yet the laws of Israel reflect quite a different heart that challenged the prevailing culture. Why the differences? The Bible itself makes it clear that Israel often wanted to be like other cultures. Their desire for a king (1 Sam. 8:7–8)—an implicit rejection of God—and their building of a golden calf are two famous examples. Unsurprisingly then, *some* overlap with the surrounding cultures existed, though Israel had more in common with Babylon than Assyria. The Old Testament does not explicitly mention women seeking divorce, but it would not be unrealistic to expect that some divorces could be sought by women in certain circumstances, as was common in some areas of the ancient Near East. But contrary to the other nations' laws, Israel's laws did not treat women as the property of their fathers or husbands but as individuals created in God's image, people for whom he cared. As such, they were not commodities to be traded, but a vulnerable class of equals meant to be protected.

As Richard Davidson points out, while Israel exists within a broader patriarchal world, the authority that a father had over his children was not analogous to a husband-wife relationship. Rather, when we look at the Old Testament "patriarchs," we see that they were "without exception married to a powerful matriarch, and their marital relationships were functionally nonhierarchical and egalitarian." While there is some debate as to whether a patriarchal society is always necessarily synonymous with women's oppression, "the OT patriarchal system does not imply a husband's authority over his wife." While the Old Testament depicts a society in which wives are subordinated to husbands, the innate equality of the sexes pulses throughout Israel's Scriptures in a way that is completely absent from surrounding cultures.[12] We feel this pulse within Israelite laws that make it unlawful to do the things that would drive a woman to seek a divorce. In particular, sexual relationships were considered sacred and, ideally, monogamous. Throughout the Bible, adultery is equated with that most heinous of sins—idolatry. Israel belonged to one God and, likewise, one person belonged to one spouse. Both Babylon and Assyria allowed for prostitution, but because Israel believed women bear the image of God and that the monogamous covenant reflected their covenant with God, prostitution was strictly prohibited. This in turn limited the opportunities available for men to engage in adultery while emphasizing the sacredness of sexuality, elevating women's bodies above mere commodities.[13]

Still, one might argue that the Mosaic law does not prohibit male promiscuity but only female promiscuity. Reading the law carefully reveals the error in assuming there was divinely sanctioned male promiscuity in Israel. Hurley shows how the Old Testament's express prohibitions against female promiscuity and prostitution actually worked to prohibit male promiscuity as well. Here's how:

1. The law teaches that a woman could not have sexual relations with anyone other than her husband (Deut. 22:22).
2. Even a betrothed woman whose union had not yet been consummated could not have an intimate relationship with another man. Men having sex with an engaged or married woman was a capital offense for both the man and the woman (Deut. 22:23–24).
3. A man would be penalized for having sex with an unengaged girl (Ex. 22:16–17) or for selling a daughter into prostitution (Lev. 19:29; 21:9).
4. In contrast to surrounding cultures, prostitution was prohibited in Israel (Deut. 23:17–18).[14]

All of this may appear as prohibitions against what women could or could not do, but a closer look raises the question, what woman would a man be justified in having sexual relations with? The answer is none but his wife. As Hurley puts it, "While the law does not speak directly to the promiscuous man, neither does it leave him any legitimate partners."[15]

A MATTER MOST SENSITIVE

In the early 2000s, a student group invited me to speak and walked me through the halls of the university building to a showcase that had been erected by the campus secular student group. The Bible featured prominently in the display, but not in a complimentary way. Next to it was a plaque that declared, "FALSE," accompanied by Bible passages that seemed to give men mere wrist slaps for using and abusing women while also forcing women to marry their abusers. Offered as liberating alternatives to the Bible were Sam Harris's book *The End of Faith* and Richard Dawkins's *The God Delusion*, next to a plaque that endorsed them as "TRUE."

The display was meant to shock the observer, but equally shocking was its misuse and mischaracterization of Scripture. Of course, the Bible has been misused by some men to justify treating women as second-class citizens or even possessions. The passages in that display likely have served as the springboard for some to justify that abuse, however, not because they were properly understood, but because they were misunderstood. We tread carefully here, though. In light of the genuine sensitivity necessary when talking about rape, any explanation of biblical passages and their contexts showing that they don't condone such behavior can risk appearing either aloof or overly defensive. While I believe such explanations are important and true, we must never minimize what some have suffered.

With this sensitivity in mind, let's take a closer look at how the Bible addresses women and sexual interactions with men compared with Israel's ancient Near Eastern neighbors. The contrasts are revealing.

In Middle Assyrian laws, if a virgin was raped by a married man, the virgin's father could take the married man's wife and have her raped. Apart from this exception, however, if someone raped a married woman, he would be put to death. What jumps out at us from these Middle Assyrian laws is that they do not penalize the dishonor done to the sanctity of a woman's body, but the dishonor done to her father or her husband. The woman in each of these situations became a stigmatized burden to her father and husband for the rest of her days.[16] But in Israel, as Jacob Milgrom notes, "there was no stigma attached to a raped (or seduced) single girl."[17] Much has been written on internet blogs about what the Old Testament says about rape. Yet most of these critiques are stuck at a surface-level reading, failing to dig behind the English translation into the original meaning of the Hebrew text; nor do they seek to understand the historical, cultural, and literary context in which these statements were written. But as scholar Richard Davidson points out, "Never is there any hint in Scripture that the rape victim is assigned guilt."[18] Indeed, the Old Testament law imposed a severe legal penalty for the perpetrator of rape, rather than scapegoating the woman. By contrast, ancient Near Eastern customs would allow—and even encourage—the raping of female captives taken in war. In Israel, by contrast, the foreign captive could be fully integrated into Israelite society, indicating that no woman, Israelite or not, could be treated as a sex object.[19] God is depicted in various ways as the protector of the vulnerable.

The display I saw at this university decrying the Bible as false referenced passages in the Bible that—at a surface level—seem to force a woman who was raped to marry her rapist, citing (if memory serves) Deuteronomy 22:23–29. But a careful reading of those passages shows that this is a gross mischaracterization. The passages require the deaths of both parties in the case of adultery (not rape) and prescribe lifelong financial penalties for a man who seduces with some level of force falling short of rape. Regardless of whether such a man would be considered a seducer or a rapist, he is required to marry the woman and financially support her his entire life, without possibility of release from that obligation. Why? Because in that culture and at that time, women were (for the most part) not financially independent. Any woman who had a sexual encounter of any kind was very unlikely to find a husband. If her seducer or rapist was put to death, she might never have any support, condemning her to a life of poverty or something worse. But to be clear—the Bible does not require the woman to marry her seducer or rapist. She had a choice to marry him and receive financial support for life. And it's possible she might be free of the obligation to live with him in such a scenario. She could also refuse marriage altogether and live supported by her father, demanding that her seducer/rapist pay the customary dowry for that support.[20] The takeaway from this is that even in brutal cultural circumstances, God opposed abuse of every type—whether it was spousal abuse, oppression of the poor, or taking advantage of the widow—and pointed the world toward a greater ideal and harmony, which was shown to us in Christ and will be fully realized in the age to come.

God wants to protect the hearts and bodies of his people, which is what the Mosaic law intended within its historical and cultural context. In that time, single women were vulnerable prey, especially if they were divorced or widowed. God implements laws and rules that limit divorces and protect widows. These laws may not always appear to be ideal by our contemporary standards, but we need to account for the reality of life in other times and cultures. Ideal laws change based on the unique circumstances and pitfalls that await the vulnerable in a society. Davidson notes that this realization is now coming to light in that "more current research in pentateuchal law . . . . is revealing that the legislation that at first sight appears to relegate women to a lower status was instead intended as a protective measure for the more vulnerable members of society, particularly for women and those who were physically disadvantaged."[21] Unfortunately, space prohibits a full treatment of these thorny issues and texts, but helpful books are available to guide you in this study.[22]

WOMEN IN THE NEW TESTAMENT WORLD

If ideals for protecting the vulnerable and elevating women to their rightful status progress as culture progresses, why does there appear to be no such progress in the New Testament period, hundreds of years after the Old Testament period? When we compare the seemingly steep curve of progress women have made in a post-Christian culture to the relatively flat curve between the two biblical periods, one might conclude that the Bible acted as progress's shackles. But is this true?

When we examine the Mediterranean region contemporary with the New Testament era, we find very little improvement in women's status and rights—except in the Christian context. For the ancient Greeks, most women were little more than chattel property with no power in public or private life. They were vessels for offspring or objects of male pleasure. As in the ancient societies already mentioned, a man's wife belonged to him alone, but unmarried and married men could consort with male or female prostitutes.[23] In ancient Rome, if women weren't seen as mere chattel, they were still under the authority of their fathers and their husbands. While women had a higher standing within the household in Roman culture, they were still forbidden from divorcing their husbands. Men, however, were free to engage in extramarital affairs. Upper-class women in Roman society were privy to some higher social benefits (while still belonging to their husbands), but lower-class women did not have access to the protection money could buy.[24] Recall the aforementioned historian Tom Holland, whose search for the roots of modern morality in Roman culture led him to discover that the Roman system was "almost every way . . . a world that is unspeakably cruel to our way of thinking."[25]

Even in the Jewish world contemporary to the New Testament, we find mixed messages about women's equality. In 190 BC Jesus Ben Sirach wrote of a spiteful wife, "No wickedness comes anywhere near the wickedness of a woman."[26] The Talmud has a general attitude "reflected in its frequently classing women with children and (Gentile) slaves,"[27] Rabbi Judah ben Elai wrote in the second century about three blessings a man should say each day, the second of which was "[Blessed art thou] who has not made me a woman."[28] Reflecting an attitude that persists in the Middle East even to this day, the Talmud also states that while "the world cannot exist without males and females—happy is he whose children are males, and woe to him whose children are females."[29]

One particularly important rabbi named Eliezer, mentioned in the Talmud, was a strong opponent of women attending religious services with men and went so far as to prohibit women from learning God's law at all. He once dismissed a woman's question on the interpretation of a passage, since "there is no wisdom in women except with the distaff [spindle]."[30] A version of this story preserved in the earlier Jerusalem Talmud adds that Eliezer's son, Horquenos, was upset with his father since the woman was paying Horquenos to teach her the law. Eliezer coldly responded, "It is better that the words of the Law should be burned than that they should be given to a woman [much less be given to her for money's sake]."[31]

Contemporary with the apostle Paul, the influential Hellenistic Jewish thinker Philo of Alexandria wrote that a man's attitude is formed from reason, but a woman's from sensuality.[32] And Josephus, the famed Jewish historian to the Romans, stated much more curtly, "The woman is inferior to the man in every way."[33]

Given this cultural backdrop and the fact that the New Testament was written mostly by Jews like Paul, a "Hebrew of Hebrews" and a "Pharisee" in his own words (Phil. 3:5), we would expect to find the same nails-on-a-chalkboard sentiments within its pages. Some passages, on a superficial reading, seem to provide evidence of just that. In Ephesians 5:22–24 Paul wrote that wives are to submit to their husbands "for the husband is the head of the wife even as Christ is the head of the church." In 1 Corinthians 14:33–35 Paul seemed to admonish women to keep silent in churches and learn in submission to their husbands at home, because "it is shameful for a woman to speak in church." He also wrote in 1 Timothy 2:11–15 that women are to "learn quietly with all submissiveness," going so far as to say, "I do not permit a woman to teach or to exercise authority over a man" because "Adam was not deceived, but the woman was deceived and became a transgressor." Some feminists, Kathy Keller tells us, refer to these and other verses as "texts of terror."[34] While a surface reading may lead to consternation, a deeper look alleviates our concerns.

THE FOUR CORNERS OF INTERPRETATION

Fondness and anxiety simultaneously frame my memories of law school, including my first course—contract law. Doubtless an illustration drawn from a course in contract law won't spark the neurons in your brain to fire with intrigue, but I ask you to bear with me. What I learned there has overflowed the banks of my law practice to water my efforts at understanding other viewpoints and, of course, my efforts to understand the Bible.

A key principle of contract interpretation dictates that phrases and clauses should be given their plain and obvious meaning, especially when they appear unambiguous. Many times, however, a clause that might seem perfectly clear on its surface actually means something else within the document's broader context or the circumstances surrounding how and why the contract was agreed to in the first place. Jurists interpret contractual language by looking at the "four corners of the document"—meaning the entire context of what it communicates, rather than myopically focusing on just one clause or phrase. In some cases, courts look to external factors, like how the parties performed the contract in the past, to decipher what the contract really means. It is sometimes the case that a contract seems internally contradictory, one clause seeming to grant to a party what another clause takes away. In other words, courts assume that the drafter of a contract wasn't deliberately or even mistakenly contradictory. Indeed, it's often the case that when this principle is applied and the entire context is considered, troubling or even conflicting contractual clauses bring to light clear-cut solutions to complex issues. Applying the same principles to the New Testament passages, specifically the so-called texts of terror, reveals that the Bible conveys much more subtlety and complexity about gender roles and authority than a superficial reading allows.

Now, employing those principles doesn't necessarily yield a single interpretation of what Paul meant. In fact, various traditions take the Bible seriously, employ the same interpretive techniques, yet come to differing conclusions. Allow here a moment's pause to survey the various views that have arisen from interpreting what the Bible says about gender roles and equality. One tradition is known as *complementarianism*, which is the view that men and women are equal in worth but have distinct roles in the church and the household such that women cannot lead men or have authority over them in those contexts. *Egalitarianism* is the view that the sexes have equal worth and that women can occupy roles of authority in the church and households, even over men. This is an extremely simplified survey of these views, and my intention is not to explain comprehensively or to defend either view or its variations. It is important, however, to note that these differing views exist among faithful followers of Christ.[35] Regardless of their varied finish lines on gender roles, these views share the same starting line on gender equality. Complementarians, egalitarians, and all those in between overwhelmingly affirm the ontological equality of women and men.

Scholars across these traditions rightly see inherent conflicts between wooden interpretations of passages like Ephesians 5:22–24; 1 Corinthians 14:33–35; and 1 Timothy 2:11–15 to mean that women are inferior to men and must not speak in church, and numerous other passages written by Paul and other apostles that women do, in fact, have the authority to teach, have taught, and have even spoken on God's behalf as prophets (see Acts 18:26; 21:9; 1 Cor. 11:5; 2 Tim. 1:5; 3:15; and Titus 2:3–4). Put in legal interpretation terms, exegetes of the various views look to the four corners of Scripture and evidence surrounding the writing of these passages to determine what Paul meant.

Now, one could make the uncharitable assumption that Paul contradicted both Jesus and himself (or that Paul may have written some passages but not the others). The more reasonable alternative, however, is to assume neither conflict nor contradiction, but to see whether other factors harmonize all of what Paul was communicating. I suggest that the very fact that the various interpretive views take the Bible seriously enough to reject superficial understandings that relegate women to second-class citizens or property speaks volumes against the charge that Christianity inherently devalues women.

With this crucial interpretive backdrop in mind, let us search the context and four corners of the New Testament landscape to discover women's prominence and equality within its pages.

SEARCHING THE CONTEXT AND FOUR CORNERS TO FIND THE TRUTH

Looking to the four corners of Paul's life and what he said about women reveals that his writings are saturated with references to and commendations of bold, wise, and respected women. In Acts 17, for example, we learn that "quite a few prominent women" joined Paul and Silas on their journeys (v. 4 NIV). In Romans 16 Paul listed several people he considered significant in the church's development and the gospel's propagation. He specifically named women, calling them deacons, coworkers, hard workers, and friends. He began by commending Phoebe (vv. 1–2), whom Paul entrusted to deliver the book of Romans to the Christians there. Michael Bird spotlights the fact that Paul entrusted a woman to deliver what would become the most influential theological treatise in history.

Paul also mentioned Priscilla and Aquila, a married couple and his "co-workers," of whom he wrote, "Not only I but all the churches of the Gentiles are grateful to them" (vv. 3–4 NIV). Priscilla and Aquila both taught the gospel message to Apollos, who would become an influential and charismatic evangelist and church leader in Corinth (Acts 18:26).[36] A small but significant detail nestles in the shrubbery of Romans 16—Paul listed Priscilla's name (Prisca) before Aquila's, which was unusual for that time and points to her prominence in the early church.[37] Similarly in Romans 16:7, Paul greeted Andronicus and Junia, who is most likely a woman, and says that they are both well known to the apostles. Verse 7 may even be translated as Junia being included among the apostles.[38] In his epistle to the Philippians, Paul mentioned both Euodia and Syntyche, two women who "have labored side by side with me in the gospel" (Phil. 4:2–3). When writing a second letter to his protégé Timothy, Paul credited and specifically named Timothy's mother Eunice and grandmother Lois for Timothy's strong faith (2 Tim. 1:5).

The point is that neither the New Testament in general nor specifically Paul downplays the pivotal roles women played in the early church as supporters, coworkers, and perhaps as leaders and educators—even educators of some of the early church's most influential men. In just these few examples, we see an impassable chasm between the Bible's words and the rabbinic tradition.

FIXING THE BLAME

A subtle yet important posture within Paul's writings also sets him apart from the sexist leanings of his rabbinic contemporaries. It was not uncommon for Jewish theologians and rabbis to blame Eve— not Adam—for humanity's fall from Eden.[39] One would expect the Pharisee Paul to fall in line with his fellow rabbis. He knew the depiction of the fall in Genesis 3 well and thus was aware of Eve's role in that catastrophic turn of events. And yet Paul flipped the script, writing that "sin entered the world through one *man*," and that "death reigned through that one *man*" (Rom. 5:12, 17 NIV, emphasis added). It is in Adam, not Eve, that "all die" (1 Cor. 15:22). When Paul wrote in 1 Timothy 2:14 that Eve was the one deceived into doing that which was forbidden by God, he implied that while Eve was misled into sin, Adam didn't need the serpent's deceptions to motivate his own rebellion.[40] Characterizing Eve as deceived may present a danger, says Philip Payne, because it may imply that women are gullible and therefore less worthy of authority. But the text does not sustain that implication. Instead, Paul was using the deception of Eve to address a particular situation brewing in the particular community to which he wrote 1 Timothy: women being deceived by a certain false teaching. "Like Eve," Payne writes, "women in Ephesus were the target of false teachers, 'who worm their way into homes and gain control over weak-willed women' (2 Tim 3:6–9)." Perhaps in a culture where women weren't considered all that important, Paul was pointing out that deceived women can—just like deceived men (2 Tim. 3:13; Titus 3:3)—wreak havoc on communal unity.[41] Paul's concern for the influence of women in the fledgling church is yet another hint at his view of women's importance and equality in distinction to his contemporaries' low view of women.

TACKLING THE TEXTS OF TERROR

Ephesians 5:22: Women and Submission to Men?

In light of the foregoing ways in which Paul highlighted women's prominence and equality, how do we make sense of Paul's words in Ephesians 5:22–24? Those verses read, "Wives, submit to your own husbands, as to the Lord. For the husband is the head of the wife even as Christ is the head of the church, his body, and is himself its Savior. Now as the church submits to Christ, so also wives should submit in everything to their husbands." Scanning the four corners would quickly bring us to the immediately preceding verse, Ephesians 5:21, which admonishes men *and* women to submit "to *one another* out of reverence for Christ" (emphasis added). This mutual submission forms the backdrop for what it means for a wife to submit to her husband. Indeed, the Greek word for "submit" is not actually found in Ephesians 5:22. Instead, it is found in verse 21. Reading the English translations, we are naturally tempted to sample verse 22 without seasoning it by verse 21, which flavors the other verses with the loving and willing mutual submission needed for any marriage to survive.

Two considerations sustain this point. First, logically, a call for the wife to submit does not mean that there will never be any call for the husband to submit, just as we would not say that the call for husbands to love their wives (v. 25) somehow precludes wives from loving their husbands.[42] Second, Paul directed husbands to subject their interests to their wives' welfare. Paul challenged men with these words: "Husbands, love your wives, just as Christ loved the church and gave himself up for her to make her holy, cleansing her by the washing with water through the word" (vv. 25–26 NIV). Accordingly, wives are called to lovingly and willingly be in subjection to their husbands, who in turn are called to promote their wives' flourishing through loving self-sacrifice, even of their own lives. Husbands, in being called to reflect Christ's character, are called to serve their wives, just like Jesus who "did not come to be served, but to serve" (Matt. 20:28; Mark 10:45 NIV).[43]

A Christian man dare not gloss over this key element of his marital covenant. It would be a misuse of Holy Writ to stop at "wives submit" and forget the rest of Paul's instruction. Hurley uses Ephesians 5:21–25 to sting men who are "overly concerned" to "maintain their authority" over their wives. Such husbands, Hurley notes, may describe the freedom they experience in praying to God, confessing anything to him to whom they've submitted without fear of angry rebuke. Yet, Hurley laments, "It is a pity that their actual relations with their spouses are frequently not in line with their Master's example and produce opposite effects."[44] This calls me back to those days of premarital counseling with my wife, Nicole. I was counseled that any authority I have is subject to her welfare. In that symbiosis, we both are privileged to reflect at least something of the one who came "not to be served, but to serve" and provide for our ultimate flourishing.

When a husband falls short of this standard, Scripture provides him a remedial path—through the conduct of his wife that mirrors what he should have been doing. In 1 Peter 3:1–2, we read, "Wives, *in the same way*, accept the authority of your husbands, so that, even if some of them do not obey the word, they may be won over without a word by their wives' conduct, when they see the purity and reverence of your lives" (NRSV, emphasis added). Behold for at least a moment how the beauty of adorning oneself with Christ can act as a beacon, calling the husband home to mutual service in marriage. What's more, the four corners of Scripture illuminate the depths of meaning. Peter called wives to submit to their husbands "in the same way" (1 Peter 3:1). But in the same way as what? The preceding verse tells us: in a way that reflects Jesus' world-altering sacrifice and compassion (1 Peter 2:21–25).[45]

I Corinthians 14:33b–35 and I Timothy 2:11–15: Silencing Women?

And so we arrive at the seemingly insurmountable "texts of terror." Does 1 Corinthians 14:33b–35 demand the complete silence of women in church? The passage reads:

> As in all the churches of the saints, the women should keep silent in the churches. For they are not permitted to speak, but should be in submission, as the Law also says. If there is anything they desire to learn, let them ask their husbands at home. For it is shameful for a woman to speak in church.

Similarly, does 1 Timothy 2:8–15 dictate women's complete silence and how they dress or wear their hair? That passage reads:

> I desire then that in every place the men should pray, lifting holy hands without anger or quarreling; likewise also that women should adorn themselves in respectable apparel, with modesty and self-control, not with braided hair and gold or pearls or costly attire, but with what is proper for women who profess godliness—with good works. Let a woman learn quietly with all submissiveness. I do not permit a woman to teach or to exercise authority over a man; rather, she is to remain quiet. For Adam was formed first, then Eve; and Adam was not deceived, but the woman was deceived and became a transgressor. Yet she will be saved through childbearing—if they continue in faith and love and holiness, with self-control.

When discussing these texts, Kathy Keller urges us to keep a few things in mind. These passages cannot be blanket prohibitions on women speaking in church. Just three chapters before the 1 Corinthians 14 passage, Paul describes how women are to prophesy and pray in church. Not only do prophecy and prayer necessitate speaking, but prophecy is itself an authoritative act of speaking on behalf of God himself. In other words, Paul can't be condemning something he just condoned. In fact, Keller points out that in the case of the 1 Corinthians passage, Paul had earlier in the very same book ranked the gift of prophecy—which women are able to do—as higher than the gift of teaching (see 1 Cor. 12:28).[46]

What, then, is going on in these texts? How are we to reconcile what seem like contradictions within Paul's writings? Looking to the four corners and the cultural context clears the path to harmonization. If we won't allow for that, skepticism may mutate into cynicism. A skeptic doesn't believe a claim until there's good evidence to substantiate it. A cynic is someone who won't believe a claim even when there is such evidence.

To satisfy the skeptic, some have argued that the so-called texts of terror are really texts of tempering. In other words, they are not universal statements or blanket prohibitions. Rather, these texts applied to specific situations in specific churches at specific times. Throughout his letters, Paul refers to specific situations he or his audience face. That context straightens out passages that at first seem askew when read with only our context in mind. First Corinthians was a letter Paul wrote specifically to the fledgling church in Corinth. While the principles Paul was inspired to pen in that letter have universal application, he doubtless had to address issues specific and unique to that church. Likewise, Paul wrote 1 Timothy specifically to the new church at Ephesus, which faced its own challenges. Again, what Paul wrote to them has timeless application in principle even as he gave instruction about circumstances specific to first-century Ephesian Christians.

Examining these texts within the four corners of Paul's words, the surrounding circumstances, and even the corpus of the New Testament uncovers helpful patterns. Some parts of the passages are specific to that time and place, while other passages, such as 1 Corinthians 11:5—which describes women prophesying in church—apply much more broadly. The specific context shouldn't give us the impression that these letters don't apply to us today and are thus irrelevant. Rather, the fact that the Scriptures applied so specifically to the past while simultaneously offering profound truths to us today hints at their timeless inspiration.

In both 1 Corinthians 14 and 1 Timothy 2, Paul was trying to extinguish flames erupting from the embers of chaotic heresies and sexually suggestive dress in Corinth and Ephesus. The church in Corinth had enthusiastically received the gospel message yet was heavy-laden with moral and cultural baggage. The assembly at Corinth had a few Jewish converts but consisted mostly of Gentile converts from paganism. Licentiousness, gossip, and classism leached the spiritual progress out of the Corinthian body of believers. False teachers easily influenced the anemic church, causing them to elevate mysticism over propositional truth. Something similar was happening in Ephesus, where a sexual revolution among women had begun, encouraging immodest dress to signal sexual availability and encouraging childlessness as liberation. The story of Eve in the garden of Eden was being recast to fit a new narrative that raising children was somehow enslavement.[47]

What was necessary in Corinth and Ephesus wasn't just regulation, but a trained clergy that could guide the congregation in expressing their spirituality responsibly and in a way that witnessed to Christ's love for the world. Suffice it to say, there was a lot at stake. Kathy Keller puts it this way: "False doctrine was the biggest enemy of the infant church, and the counter to it was to have a group of local elders, chosen for their maturity in the faith, whose job it was to judge truth from heresy."[48] The trained clergy at that time and place were men. Yes, the women could have been (and some were) trained and educated. But the exigencies of the circumstances dictated that a young church be led by those qualified to do so, and at this point in time, it just so happened to be men. Of course, men were no more immune then than they are now to being misled into false teaching. Indeed, Paul's letter warning of false teaching was directed to men as much as to women.

But, one might argue, the text in 1 Corinthians 14 itself shows that Paul was not writing to address issues specific to the Corinthian church. The verse reads, after all, that "As in all the churches of the saints, the women should keep silent" (1 Cor. 14:33b–34). True, some English translations group "As in all the churches" and "women should keep silent" in the same verse. But that grouping isn't the only translational option. The chapter and verse conventions we are familiar with today are relatively new inventions, meant to facilitate Bible reading. In the oldest and best manuscripts, however, there were no chapter or verse numbers. Because the manuscripts include neither spaces between words nor punctuation, scholars have to determine whether a verse should include a particular sentence or phrase that could have been paired with another sentence or phrase. Occasionally they disagree. First Corinthians 14:33a–b is one such occasion. Responsible scholars have opted, with good reason, to link the phrase "as in all the churches" with verse 33a instead of 33b, such that the verse reads, "For God is not a God of confusion, but of peace, as in all the churches of the saints. . ." (1 Cor. 14:33 NASB; see also NIV). This would make sense since Paul clearly, within the very same letter to the Corinthians just a few chapters before, mentioned that women pray and prophesy (speak authoritatively) (1 Cor. 11:5). But even if "As in all the churches" should be linked to "women should keep silent," one could see that Paul was probably not prohibiting women from speaking at all, but from speaking in a manner that usurped a teaching authority they had not yet earned and spread heresy.

In 1 Timothy, Paul addressed women's hairstyles in the church at Ephesus for reasons specific to that congregation. Hurley notes that Paul was not trying to control how women dressed in general. Rather, his concern was with the types of hairstyles that spoke to socioeconomic class distinctions that brought division within the nascent church. In Ephesus the wealthy and high-class prostitutes wore similar hairstyles, which were "enormously elaborate arrangements with braids and curls interwoven or piled high like towers and decorated with gems and/or gold and/or pearls."[49] Paul was not singling out women for the way they dressed but instead was using the situation in Ephesus to discourage the church from becoming a cavalcade of wealth flaunting, much like the sinful world around them. This principle could easily apply to men just as much as women.

Other scholars agree that Paul was not making universal statements here. Further, the elaborate hairstyles may have been linked to false teachings. The adornment of these women, Philip Towner argues, was associated with the transgression of sexual mores and the rejection of traditional family roles and structures such as childbearing.[50] Second, Towner posits a situation in which certain wealthy women were embracing and promulgating a "heretical teaching."[51] Thus, the prohibition against women teaching was rather specific to that historical and social situation. Therefore, 1 Timothy 2:11–12 does not contradict Romans 16:1–7 or Acts 18:24–28 and does not represent a blanket statement made by Paul applying to all women everywhere for all time. According to Ben Witherington, 1 Timothy 2:11–12 contains no "universal prohibition of women speaking in church."[52] Witherington also detects evidence that Paul was responding to a situation of "women being involved in false teaching and being led astray into apostasy."[53]

One symptom of this false teaching might have been its hubris (as seen in its connection to upper-class dress), which is why Paul wrote in 1 Timothy 2:12 that he did not permit a woman to "exercise authority" over a man. Scholar Philip Payne asserts that this most likely means something more like "to assume authority," which means to take what has not (yet, at least) been earned.[54] Linda Belleville has argued persuasively for the terms *dominating* or *domineering power.*[55] In this sense, it was a specific prohibition against false teaching leading to seizing of authority neither given nor earned through proper training.

Of course, this leaves open the matter of female ordination, an issue that has been debated for centuries and one I won't pretend to be able to solve in a few paragraphs. Yet allow me to offer this: I have had the blessing of being surrounded by female colleagues so very gifted at communicating with poise, humility, intelligence, and compassion that I've wondered why I am even sharing a platform with them. Regardless of the question of their ordination, God has provided them with an outlet for their gifts.

WOMEN WHO STOOD OUT BY BEING HIDDEN IN CHRIST

The Bible is rife with women of courage and gifts that changed the course of history. They have inspired women like my colleagues and friends to speak on important issues, not the least of which is the way Jesus championed women's equality. Between the first century and today, we find women whose valor was inspired by biblical women. I think of Amy Carmichael, the missionary who served in India and never married. She needed no man's approval for her validation save one—Jesus of Nazareth. She is credited as saying that before she would ever marry a man, she wanted her life to be so "in Christ" that any man had to encounter Jesus on the route to her heart. She and so many others like her read the pages of the Bible, both Old and New Testaments, and found their value in the depths of its verses. The Bible empowered them to set the terms of their lives on the divine authority that comes with giving Jesus top priority. Our focus now turns to the way the Word of God points to God the Word made flesh—the Man who championed women.

CHAPTER 7

WHEN GOD PUTS WOMEN IN THEIR PLACE

AN INTIMIDATING INVITATION

Itinerant speaking has afforded me the privilege of encountering people from diverse ethnic and religious backgrounds. Yet I'm perpetually fascinated by the fact that cultures separated by thousands of miles and many centuries can be so similar. One would think that the differences between Middle Eastern culture and Peruvian culture would be as wide as the miles that separate Peru and Lebanon. Having visited Peru numerous times now, I've learned that, just like Arabs, Peruvians don't have much regard for being on time, value large families, practice an almost obnoxious hospitality, and express love through food. And like the Lebanese, Peruvians consider their cuisine a matter of well-earned pride—and with good reason. Peruvians occupy a special place in my heart. I've often quipped when I'm in Peru that being among them is like being among Arabs who speak Spanish.

A charming and simultaneously disconcerting commonality among the cultures is their willingness to impose short-notice itinerary changes on the unsuspecting. Our hosts in Lima were skilled at surfing unforeseen waves coming from inviting hosts, which ensured that we were never bored. Having made several trips to Peru, I was becoming quite confident in my ability to adapt the content and tone of a talk meant for university students that would unexpectedly have to be delivered instead to lawyers and judges. On one particular trip, however, my hosts discovered a way to shatter that growing confidence.

Just days before I was to arrive in Peru, my colleagues there contacted me about a scheduling change. Hearing of another last-minute schedule change was not a surprise to me or my assistant. The change of audience, however, was a different matter. Instead of speaking to university students or groups of businesspeople, I was being asked to speak at a conference, a major conference. A women's conference.

Had they given me a thousand guesses, I would have used all of them before the words "Peruvian Women's Conference" would have parted my lips.

As a lawyer, I learned to utilize an effective poker face. "Sounds interesting," I said nonchalantly to my assistant under my breath even as my pulse quickened. She smiled because she could read past the poker face. To hide my panic, I resorted to sarcasm. "Naturally, they'd ask *me* to speak at a women's conference," I let out. "Who's more suited to address a thousand Peruvian women about their female identity in Christ than a former Muslim, American-born, Lebanese man?"

I had to prepare for numerous events in Peru, but the women's conference dominated my thoughts. Research usually calms my nerves, as unknowns become known, so I did a little research on the state of women's affairs in Peru. Among many things, I learned that Peruvian women are passionate, are fiercely loyal to their families, are typically religious, and are now finding increased influence in the professional world. *Whew*, I thought, *at least they are somewhat similar to Middle Eastern women.* But another piece of information roped my anxiety back in. Within Peru there lurks a disconcerting acceptance of spousal abuse, even when it occurs in public. That, too, is an unfortunate commonality with the Middle East. Yet in my own experience living in the West and having a strong, loving family, I had no experience or exposure to these harsh realities. I started to panic. What could I possibly offer these Peruvian women about identity and hope, given what so many had undoubtedly gone through? What experience could I draw from? I wracked my brain for an answer and then arrived at two people whose lives would prove to be founts of wisdom and experience from which I could offer at least something of value to a group of women whose lives I knew so little about. The first person was not a woman, but a man. And, of course, that man was Jesus.

NO TOKENS

"[It] will not be taken away from her."

Jesus uttered these words during an encounter with two women. The account is familiar to most Christians, but the revolutionary power of these words gets lost in the familiarity.

Jesus and his disciples had been invited to the house of a woman named Martha who had a sister named Mary. Luke's gospel records that while Martha was busy with meal preparations and the activities a hospitable Middle Eastern woman would be expected to do, her sister, Mary, wasn't helping at all. Instead, Mary "sat at the Lord's feet and listened to his teaching" (Luke 10:39). Mary was not acting like a typical Middle Easterner, let alone a Middle Eastern woman. She should have been frantic with worry about whether there was enough food for the guests and whether the house was clean enough. Yet there she was, sitting at Jesus' feet along with his male disciples, hanging on every word he uttered. *How shameful!* Martha may have thought. *Who does my little sister think she is? A candidate for rabbi? A position only a man can hold?*

Martha was no shrinking violet, and she let her opinion be known. "Lord," she said to Jesus, "don't you care that my sister has left me to do the work by myself? Tell her to help me!" (Luke 10:40 NIV). Jesus' response was short but bursting with meaning. "Martha, Martha, you are worried and upset about many things, but few things are needed—or indeed only one. Mary has chosen what is better, and *it will not be taken away from her*" (vv. 41–42 NIV, emphasis added).

In countless sermons in countless churches, pastors have used this story to illustrate the general idea that any one of us can be so distracted with worries, anxiety, busyness, and even our own sense of duty that we fail to pause and focus on cultivating a relationship with Jesus. Martha wanted to serve Jesus, while Mary wanted to honor him. That is indeed a valuable and true lesson to draw from the encounter at Martha's home. But there is much more to be found in this account. I'm convinced that Jesus was also deliberately speaking about the value of women and their right to an education.

Some time ago I was introduced to a fascinating podcast by

bestselling author Malcolm Gladwell titled *Revisionist History*. Gladwell describes it as a podcast "about things overlooked and misunderstood." You may not agree with everything he says on the podcast, but it is quite fascinating listening. I recall listening to an episode while mowing my lawn one day that caused me to pause and rewind more than once. It was called "The Hug Heard Round the World," and it referenced the time that famed African American entertainer Sammy Davis Jr. hugged presidential nominee Richard Nixon at the Republican National Convention.[1] It was a hug that nearly devastated Davis's career. He was labeled a traitor to his race for embracing Nixon, who was all but openly racist. Much of the podcast episode was thought provoking as it explored the idea of Sammy Davis Jr.'s need to be loved by white people—even though those same people readily disparaged him (under the guise of satire) for being black. A few minutes of the episode addressed how this phenomenon operates in gender contexts as well. Gladwell referenced research by Rosabeth Moss Kanter, a professor at Harvard Business School in the late 1970s, on what happened to "token" women entering the sales force of a large industrial firm. At that point, the sales force was almost entirely male. Though a handful of women had trickled in for the first time, they were struggling professionally. Dr. Kanter concluded that they were struggling—not because of their abilities—but because there weren't enough women in the sales force to offer mutual support in a field dominated by men. A typical office for that company was only eight salespeople, and only one of them (if any) was a woman. That lone woman became a token, creating a special set of problems for the woman *and* the men in that office. Men became overly lewd and aggressive, telling dirty jokes and making comments in an exaggerated fashion, while the woman—the token—found herself increasingly uncomfortable and self-conscious, which quite naturally impacted her performance. But a surprising phenomenon also occurred in such environments. To gain acceptance with the majority men, the woman eventually had to *become one of them*, mimicking their behavior and making other women who held clerical positions uncomfortable and self-conscious. Put another way, Dr. Kanter found that one of the ways "token" women tried to cope with being in an uncomfortable work environment was to turn on their own gender, joining the men in putting other women in their place, as it were.[2]

The lamentable social trend that Dr. Kanter explored helps us plumb the depths of Jesus' encounter with Martha and Mary. In Jesus' day, women were not generally afforded a complete education. Women were not allowed to study the Bible at a rabbi's feet, let alone become rabbis themselves. Yet Martha's sister, Mary, saw that she was welcome to sit at Rabbi Jesus' feet. "Sitting at the feet" of a teacher wasn't a derogatory term. In fact, any man hoping to study Torah in those days would have considered it a great honor to sit at the feet of a great teacher like Hillel, Gamaliel, or Nicodemus. Mary seized the opportunity for an otherwise elusive education by "sitting" at Jesus' feet, even if only for a short time. Mary's opportunism would have shocked her culture at large, and it certainly shocked her older sister, Martha. When we read the story, we think of Martha being irritated that her lazy sister was using Jesus' presence as an excuse not to work. And that may have been part of Martha's thinking. But it also looks like Martha was appalled that Mary had the audacity to sit at Jesus' feet and dare to get the kind of education only a man was entitled to in that culture. Martha and Mary's place was seen as the kitchen, the place a good woman should be. I firmly believe that Martha expected Jesus to side with her and put Mary in her place. Martha was so assimilated to the gender barriers in her culture that when she saw Mary breach that barrier, she criticized her, expecting Jesus' approval.

Jesus shocked Martha—as he regularly did most people—by welcoming a woman at his feet to learn from him. Jesus was appalled that women were denied an education or any of the basic rights men enjoyed at that time. Yes, Martha was being kind and hospitable as a Middle Eastern woman is prone to be. But Jesus saw that Martha's objection to Mary's sitting at his feet was more than just Mary trying to avoid work. The real tragedy was that Martha had grown so accustomed to "being put in her place" that she saw Mary's venture beyond that place as wrong. Jesus wanted to dispel the lies Martha had believed—the spell that religious men had put Martha under. Such a spell is remarkable given Scripture's repeated affirmations of women's equal worth and value, and examples of women gaining education, being in business, and having lives beyond the kitchen. Of one such women, the Bible says, "She considers a field and buys it; with the fruit of her hands she plants a vineyard. She dresses herself with strength and makes her arms strong. She perceives that her merchandise is profitable" (Prov. 31:16–18) and "Strength and dignity are her clothing, and she laughs at the time to come. She opens her mouth with wisdom, and the teaching of kindness is on her tongue" (Prov. 31:25–26).

Echoing these ancient truths, Jesus reminded Martha, "Mary has chosen what is better"—she has chosen to pursue an education forbidden by society but encouraged by the Lord—and he would not let it be taken from her. Not by the rabbis who thought teaching women was pointless and even dangerous. Not even by another woman.

This incident has had its ripple effects through history. Scholar

Diana Lynn Severance recounts the story of Paula, a wealthy Christian woman who used her wealth and influence centuries ago to educate others, including herself. She patronized Jerome's biblical translation work and barraged him with questions. Jerome praised her for her passion for knowledge. This woman Paula, Severance says, "is just one of the early demonstrations of the truth that wherever Christianity has flourished, education and the particular education of women has increased."[3] Like Jericho's walls, the barriers for at least these two women came crashing down. Their identity was not tied to their culturally imposed roles, but to their relationship with the Maker of heaven and earth.

WOMEN HEROES OF THE OLD TESTAMENT

Martha's surprise that Jesus treated her and Mary as equally deserving of an education as men is all the more tragic given that the Old Testament is riddled with stories of valiant women rising to the challenges facing their people, often at great personal risk. While likely familiar with some of the stories in the Old Testament, Martha and Mary were equally likely denied the kind of deeper education that would have revealed the Bible's description of women as teachers, prophets, and even leaders. God birthed an entire nation because of the plea of a woman named Hagar (Gen. 16:7–16). When King Josiah rediscovered the lost Book of the Law, he called on a woman named Huldah to verify the book's authenticity (2 Kings 22:14). Moses' and Aaron's sister, Miriam, was a prominent figure in Israel's exodus from Egyptian slavery. Rahab—the non-Israelite prostitute—helped Israel so much against her enemies that not only was she spared God's judgment against Jericho, but she earned a place in the New Testament's "Faith Hall of Fame" in Hebrews 11:31. And the Old and New Testaments list at least five women by name and allude to many more not specifically named as prophets who spoke on God's behalf (Ex. 15:20; Judg. 4–5; 2 Kings 22:14; Isa. 8:3; Luke 2:36; Acts 21:9). Jesus would not allow this education, this "what is better," to be taken from Martha or Mary.

I recall an intense conversation with a woman who had left Islam and become an atheist. Her journey is quite fascinating. Though committed to Islam for years, she eventually abandoned it, feeling that it had to be false because it denigrated women and didn't foster basic human rights for all people. As we conversed over the role of religion in social progress, another person who was also in our conversation asked her an important question (one that I was hoping to get the chance to ask her myself). "Do you think Christianity suffers from the same flaws? Have you ever considered Christianity as an alternative to atheism?" Her answer suggested that she had given Christianity at least a cursory glance but nothing more. Knowing that women's rights were of particular importance to her, I jumped in with a follow-up question. "Do you think Christianity fares better when it comes to women's issues?"

"I looked at Christianity a bit," she said. "But the Bible seems to oppress women just as much." That's when I listed the women who featured prominently in the biblical account of history and landed on the impressive figure of Deborah. Deborah was appointed by God himself to be a "judge," a leader within the Israelite community to make legal pronouncements over the affairs of all people, including men (Judg. 4–5). Not only that, but she was a prophet who spoke on God's behalf. The former Muslim woman was suddenly fascinated. "That's in the Bible?" she asked with genuine interest. "Where can I find this story?" She still had other issues with the biblical text, but Deborah's example served as a catalyst for better understanding. Critics who would label the Bible as sexist from cover to cover are confronted with an inconvenient truth when they truly examine the pages between those covers. "Open your Bible at random," writes Rutgers University professor Gary Rendsburg, "and you will notice something striking: Female characters abound."[4] This plethora of female figures of character and bravery is not at all what one would expect if the Bible were a mere product of patriarchy.

Two prime examples of this phenomenon in the Old Testament are the books of Ruth and Esther. Richard Bauckham points out that Ruth, a Moabite (that is, a Gentile) is viewed as a sort of "relativizing or corrective force to the lawlessness" elsewhere in the Old Testament narrative.[5] Ruth stood as an example amid a crucial transition between Israel's depraved treatment of women described in Judges 19–21 and the rekindling of God's favor toward Israel through King David. Where did this man David, who revitalized Israel's devotion to God, come from? The answer is this faithful Gentile woman—and David's great-grandmother—Ruth. Her faithfulness to her mother-in law, Naomi, and Naomi's God left an imprint on her family's DNA that would span generations.[6] So integral was she to God's redemptive plan for all humanity that the gospel of Matthew includes her in Jesus' genealogy. Indeed, in a time when the vast majority of genealogies didn't mention even a single woman, the genealogy of Jesus mentions five.

A WOMAN'S BRAVERY AND A HINT OF CHRIST

The Old Testament book titled Esther is one of the most fascinating books of the Bible for several reasons, not the least of which is its depiction of a woman who acts with awe-inspiring bravery. The gist of the book is that Esther, a Jewish girl originally born with the name Hadassah, becomes the queen of Persia and eventually saves her people from the genocidal plans masterminded by the evil sycophant Haman. As if that plotline weren't enough to show that this is a story about brave women, we also get morsels of background information pointing to not just one brave woman but to at least two.

The story opens not with Esther, but with her predecessor queen, a Persian woman of remarkable beauty named Vashti. Under Persian law of the time, no one entered the king's presence unless summoned, not even the queen. The penalty for disobedience was death. In other words, Vashti is forced to sit in separation from her husband until he beckons. The king throws a lavish banquet that lasts for days while Vashti hosts her own banquet with other women. In the middle of it all, the king summons Vashti to show her beauty to his guests. Shocking everyone, Vashti refuses his command. She will not be a mere trophy wife, no matter what the cost. The king's advisers are appalled at Vashti's insolence, fearing that when other women hear of it, they will "look at their husbands with contempt" (Esth. 1:17–18). In other words, if a woman dares to disobey the king, there will be no controlling women after that. With that, the king banishes Vashti. He selects another beautiful woman, perhaps one he thinks will be another trophy, to be his queen, the Jewish girl the Persians call Esther.

Let us not banish Vashti from our attention just yet. She has much to teach us about self-respect in the short space she occupies in Scripture. She refused to be objectified and made a spectacle for the king and his guests. She resisted what so many others before her had readily obeyed. The flames of her self-respect launched the men of Persia into a panic as they scrambled for buckets with which to dowse a wildfire of spousal rebellion. Her strength of character described in this book is particularly instructive for two reasons. First, the detail of Vashti's defiance isn't necessary to the story. Yet there it is, conspicuous in its seeming irrelevance. And second, Vashti is not a Jew, yet in this story written and told by Jews, a Persian woman's dignity introduces an account of a Jewish woman's dignity. These two realities lend both historical credibility and moral authority to the book of Esther. Had Jews been fabricating this story, they would have had little reason to chronicle Vashti's defiance—unless they were telling the story as it actually happened. The fact that this book opens with Vashti's costly act of self-respect underscores one of the themes of the book of Esther, namely, that women are not objects of desire but God's dignified image bearers.

Esther's story is a page-turner rich with detail and irony. The king's advisers thought that by banishing Vashti in favor of a new, more compliant queen, they could control women's behavior in the land. The irony is that the very replacement they called for, Esther, would disobey the king not only out of a sense of self-respect but in a demonstration of self-sacrifice for her peoples' sake.

After being selected queen, Esther learns of a plot by Haman, the king's adviser, to wipe out the Jews living in their Persian exile. She and her cousin Mordecai devise a plan to change the king's mind about the Jews and turn Haman's plot against him. The problem is that she cannot get to the king until he summons her, and time is running out before Haman's plan to exterminate the Jews is executed. Esther is faced with two options: sit idly by as her people are slaughtered while she may be spared, or risk her own life by barging into the king's presence. Mordecai fans the embers of courage he already knows lie within Esther. "Who knows whether you have not come to the kingdom for such a time as this?" he asks (4:14). In God's sovereignty, he had orchestrated Esther's royal status for a purpose. It remained up to her to act like a queen for her people's sake.

What a dance of circumstances and human will we are treated to in this story! Vashti showed her strength by refusing the king's summons. Esther prepares to show her strength by approaching the king unsummoned. A vivid picture of Esther standing in front of the king's chamber door tugs at my imagination. The human fight or flight reflex is almost overwhelming.

Her spine shudders.

She attempts deep, calming breaths, yet her lungs pulse with shallow heaves.

Adrenaline rattles her hands as she fumbles the door latches.

She presses her forehead to the doors, wondering where the strength to push them open will come from.

But she finds the strength, and the doors swing open.

With every step toward the stunned king, her echoing footsteps are drowned out by the sound of her own pulse bellowing in her ears. The king's scepter is at his side. If he extends his scepter to her, she will live. If it remains at his side, her life is forfeit and her people will perish. All hope she has for herself and the Jews rises or falls with that scepter.

Relief washes over her as he extends it. She has risked her life to execute a plan that will save her people from destruction. What a remarkable picture we get here in the Old Testament. Whereas previously we may have thought of Joseph, Moses, or Joshua as prime examples of men being the deliverers of the Israelites, here we encounter a foreign nation's queen in that celebrated position. Her plan eventually works, and God delivers the Jews through her.

It is perhaps too obvious a point to make here that God's deliverance of the Jews through Esther foreshadows God's deliverance of the world through Jesus. Esther stared down her own death to rescue her people from genocide. Jesus offered his own life to rescue the world from damnation. Esther was given the privilege of foreshadowing Christ with her self-sacrificial posture. But another detail poetically links this Jewish girl to the world's ultimate Redeemer. She turned the evil Haman's plot against him so that the king executed Haman instead of Mordecai and the Jews. By taking on the penalty for our sin, Jesus turned sin and death against themselves. The venom of sin is death—separation from God. Through the cross, death was defanged. The irony of Esther's story presaged the irony of the greatest story ever told. Esther—a woman in the Old Testament tradition—was double honored with the privilege of saving her people during her lifetime and hinting at the ultimate salvation for all people.

FEMALE METAPHORS OF THE DIVINE REALITY

Esther's foreshadowing Christ through her self-sacrificial posture isn't the only occasion in which the Bible points us to God's character through stories and references to women. Jesus famously taught valuable lessons through parables. How very Middle Eastern of him. So many of the truths I've learned in life have stuck in my mind and my heart because they were delivered to me not just through dry propositional claims, but through parables. Yes, propositional statements arranged in carefully formulated arguments can convey valuable truths. But there is something about a parable the causes those truths to lodge in our hearts more effectively. We identify with the parable's characters and put ourselves in the story. While sound arguments and propositional claims can tell us *what* the truth is, parables tell us what our *relationship* to the truth is. That is why it is particularly remarkable that on several occasions, Jesus made women the protagonists of his parables. This had two effects. First, it compelled men to think of women differently. They not only had to put themselves in a woman's place, but more pointedly, they forced men to think of women as occupying the same places as men. Second, Jesus compelled women to think of themselves differently. They could occupy the same place of prominence in God's plan for the world as any man.

Jesus' parable of the lost coin recorded in Luke 15:8–10 immediately springs to mind. "Or what woman, having ten silver coins, if she loses one coin, does not light a lamp and sweep the house and seek diligently until she finds it?" Jesus rhetorically asked his audience. "And when she has found it, she calls together her friends and neighbors, saying, 'Rejoice with me, for I have found the coin that I had lost.' Just so, I tell you, there is joy before the angels of God over one sinner who repents." That parable's fundamental lesson is that God values every person equally and will do whatever it takes to save a sinner from the consequences of sin. Yet it teaches a secondary lesson about women's equality. It was not lost on Jesus' audience, steeped in patriarchal androcentrism, that Jesus had just used a woman as an analogy for God.

Then there is the short parable of the leavened dough. In Matthew 13:33 Jesus compared the growing kingdom of God to the way a woman would mix yeast into her dough to get it to rise. "The kingdom of heaven is like leaven that a woman took and hid in three measures of flour, till it was all leavened." The woman stands as the proxy for God, who graces the dough with the ingredient needed for change and growth. What the woman does in the parable mirrors Christ's work for the kingdom of heaven.

While these are just two parables among the many that Jesus told, the fact that Jesus used women as positive examples—even as examples of God's character and work—is galactically disparate from the way rabbis roughly contemporary with Jesus spoke and wrote about women. Some of those rabbis depicted women as dangerous, seductive, irrational animals. But Jesus, in lamenting over Jerusalem's rejection of his message, employed a feminine image to illustrate God's love even for those who abandon him. "O Jerusalem, Jerusalem, the city that kills the prophets and stones those who are sent to it! How often would I have gathered your children together as a hen gathers her brood under her wings, and you were not willing!" (Luke 13:34). He incorporated women into metaphors that highlighted the character of the very God who inspired the words some rabbis refused to teach women. If that is not a poetic use of irony to teach a lesson, then I don't know what is. Jesus' women-incorporating parables and metaphors, with their shock value and spiritual depth, are photonegatives of the misogyny that soaked his culture.

FEMALE REALITIES IN THE MINISTRY OF JESUS

With the way Jesus' valued women, is it any wonder that women flocked to be a part of what he was doing in Israel? It's nearly impossible to read a page of the Gospels without coming across a woman playing a significant role in Jesus' ministry. The Gospels tell of a woman's faith compared with the skepticism of her husband even before Jesus was born. Both were devoted to God, but one—the woman—trusted God in earnest. Luke 1 tells us that an angel visited a priest named Zechariah to tell him that even though Zechariah and his wife, Elizabeth, were advanced in years and had been barren, God would bless them with a son. That son would eventually become John the Baptist. Zechariah, though a righteous man of God, doubted that this miracle could happen. As a result, he was made mute until the child was born.

Mary, the mother of Jesus, was similarly told of a miraculous birth, one that was even greater, because Mary was a virgin and would not conceive her child through marital intimacy. It is fascinating to read the differences between Mary's reaction to the angelic message and Zechariah's. Mary did not doubt the certainty of the angel's message but was naturally curious to know *how* the miracle would come about (Luke 1:34). Zechariah, however, did not ask *how* the miracle would happen, but how he could *know* that it would happen. One translation has Zechariah asking how he could "be certain." In other words, Zechariah wanted assurances before getting his hopes up. Mary, on the other hand, accepted the truth while engaging her mind to wonder at the miracle. It is fascinating that the Bible contrasts the immediate faith of a common woman with the delayed faith of a priestly man.

Jesus commended other women's faith-fueled bravery. In Matthew 15:21–28, a Canaanite woman asked Jesus to heal her daughter. Jesus engaged in educational banter with her to teach the crowd some lessons through the woman's faith. After he made his point in the hearing of the crowd, Jesus commended the faith of this non-Jewish woman. "O woman, great is your faith! Be it done for you as you desire," he told her as he healed her daughter from a distance (v. 28).

Jesus demanded that men, especially religious men, respect women. A telling example is found in Luke 7:36–50. A Pharisee (a particularly strict and austere religious leader) named Simon had invited Jesus to dinner at his home. Now, it was customary for a host to offer water to his guests with which they could wash the dust off their sandaled feet as they entered the home. Yet the Pharisee had neglected to offer this common courtesy to Jesus. Though the text doesn't make this explicit, this failure of protocol suggests that the Pharisee didn't invite Jesus to his home out of affection, but to see if he could trap Jesus into saying something controversial that could be used against him later.

As the men were reclining following the meal, a "woman of the city" burst into the house (v. 37). She began to weep in Jesus' presence, knowing that he had healed many and delivered women from oppression and sin. As she wept, she wept onto Jesus' feet, washing them with her tears and wiping them dry with her hair. She anointed Jesus' feet with a costly perfume. She had done much in her life needing forgiveness, and she found that forgiveness in Jesus. But the Pharisee was outraged. *How could Jesus be a prophet of God if he would allow such a sinner to touch him in this familiar way?*

The odor of the Pharisee's religiosity filled the room more pungently than the fragrant ointment. Simon the Pharisee had dismissed the woman as a mere annoyance. But Jesus would not dismiss her. The Bible recounts a small, specific but profound detail. Jesus confronted Simon's self-righteousness while "turning toward the woman" (v. 44). Let that sink in for a moment. He looked at the woman—not Simon—even as he spoke to Simon. "Do you see this woman?" Jesus asked him while looking at her. Simon hadn't seen *her* at all. All he saw was her sin and low station. "'I entered your house; you gave me no water for my feet, but she has wet my feet with her tears and wiped them with her hair. You gave me no kiss, but from the time I came in she has not ceased to kiss my feet. You did not anoint my head with oil, but she has anointed my feet with ointment. Therefore I tell you, her sins, which are many, are forgiven—for she loved much. But he who is forgiven little, loves little.' And he said to her, 'Your sins are forgiven'" (vv. 44–48). Jesus looked at the woman the entire time he was addressing Simon. How masterful that the simple gesture of looking at her while scolding him could simultaneously show appreciation for the woman's character and teach Simon a thing or two about his lack of humility. In a culture where women dissolved into the backgrounds of men's affairs, Jesus spotlighted the woman, speaking to her and through her.

It is no surprise, then, that in the very next verses, Luke's gospel tells us that many women, among them specifically Mary Magdalene, Joanna, and Susanna, joined Jesus in his itinerant ministry. Be careful not to miss a small but significant detail, one that forces us to reorient our misperceptions about the Bible and women. Those women not only accompanied Jesus but also financially supported his ministry out of their own means (Luke 8:1–3).

The Samaritan woman Jesus encountered at Jacob's well deserves another visit from us (John 4). Recall that she had come to the well alone when she met Jesus. That was usually because women went to retrieve water from wells in groups, for either social or safety reasons. Yet the Samaritan woman was alone. Men only associated with her, so it seemed, for their convenience. Women didn't care to associate with her out of concern for their own reputations. But not Jesus. He showed her the real well from which her true value sprang. When all others—including other women—rejected her, Jesus accepted her. The Eastern church father Ephrem the Syrian found the transformative power of what took place within the Samaritan woman at Jacob's well so powerful that he wrote, "First she caught sight of a thirsty man, then a Jew, then a Rabbi, afterwards a prophet, last of all the Messiah. She tried to get the better of the thirsty man, she showed dislike of the Jews, she heckled the Rabbi, she was swept off her feet by the prophet, and she adored the Christ."[7] Jesus did more than accept her: he sent her off to tell her village that hope in the flesh had finally come. Jesus imparted to her a truth that gave flight to her feet. She raced from the well to tell her village to drink from the fount of living water. The first cross-cultural missionary in the New Testament era was not a man, but a woman.

FROM CRADLE TO GRAVE AND BEYOND

Women played significant roles in every stage of Jesus' life. At and around his birth, women faithfully received promises and prophecies from God. Indeed, Mary, Jesus' mother, accepted a promise from God that came with a social cost. She wasn't married when the angel told her that she would conceive and give birth to a child. Surely a young woman raised in an honor-shame culture, where public shame due to even the perception of sexual sin could actually result in death, must have had not only faith but brave faith. At the very least, her parents would find it hard to believe that she got pregnant by supernatural means. Joseph, her fiancé, didn't believe it at first but was eventually convinced when an angel appeared to him. Yet we get no hint that Mary asked God why he didn't wait to bring her the child until after she was married. We see no clue that Mary's joy at being a chosen vessel of God was tainted even a bit by her worry about the inevitable social stigma that would brand her for life. Surely she felt it, but she never voiced it. The Bible records the complaints of other people—both men and women—who received good news only to worry about the shadows that would accompany the light. Why not Mary? Perhaps it was because she did not complain or worry. She trusted God, "hid these things in her heart" as it were, and endured for the sake of the gospel message to come.

The baby Mary birthed became the man to whom women would flock. They saw in him something they longed to see in others, even in themselves. One woman who had received so much from Jesus anointed him with nard that would have cost a year's wages. When others rebuked her for what seemed like waste, Jesus commended her for her thoughtfulness. He was so moved by her act that he prophesied that she would not be forgotten so long as his story would not be forgotten. Two thousand years later, I sit at a computer writing about a woman whose name I do not yet know but of whose devotion much of the world has heard or read.

Jesus described that woman's act as an anointing for his eventual burial (Matt. 26:12; Mark 14:8; John 12:7). We read that when Jesus was being beaten before his crucifixion, most of the disciples had fled. But women were there. As he hung on the cross, women remained. And after he was buried, his women followers arose early in the morning, facing the dark and the cold (both literal and metaphorical) to anoint Jesus' body for a proper burial. From cradle to grave, they honored Jesus when others were absent.

This unflappable commitment resulted in women being the first witnesses to the crowning event that would come to change the course of history: the resurrection of Jesus. All four gospels record that women were the first to be present at the empty tomb, a tomb that was supposed to be occupied by the body they had come to anoint. Matthew, Luke, and John specifically record that the women saw the resurrected Jesus. Now, this is historically significant because women's testimony was considered largely worthless in those days, at best worth half the testimony of a man. So why, if they were fabricating the story, would the gospel writers make women the primary witnesses to Jesus' resurrection? Not to shore up the story's credibility, that much is certain. No, they told the story that way because that's what happened. Had they made up the whole thing, they would have had more socially credible witnesses, like Peter, James, or John, be the first witnesses. But we find women at the empty tomb first because God, in his providence, orchestrated it that way.

The first Easter began with the first witnesses, and the first witnesses were women. And a woman was instrumental in the first Christmas, of course. These two holidays, Christmas and Easter, are the bookends between which Jesus' ministry took place. We celebrate the pageantry and gift of Christmas for months, and Easter has its special place on many calendars as well. Why celebrate Christmas? Why isn't Jesus' birth just something we commemorate and move on with like Presidents' Day in America? Because his birth wasn't just the birth of a moral teacher. His birth was the advent of Immanuel, God with us, who would live a life of such perfection that he would have no moral debts of his own to pay, enabling him to pay our collective debts on Good Friday's cross more than thirty years later. But had he died and stayed dead, we would have no way of knowing that he actually paid for anything. Not we nor the women who followed him would have hope of salvation. But Easter came, the day when hope literally and bodily rose from despair. And women were the first to behold that hope.

Christmas made Easter possible. Easter made Christmas meaningful. God graced women with the opportunity to be there for both.

Dorothy Sayers, one of the first women to earn a PhD from Oxford University, saw why women would be so attracted to Jesus that they would not only follow him at great peril but also influence their husbands to follow him. "Perhaps it is no wonder that the women were first at the Cradle and last at the Cross," she writes. They saw in Jesus a man unlike any they had ever met, a man who was "a prophet and teacher who never nagged at them, never flattered or coaxed or patronized; who never made arch jokes about them, never treated them either as 'The women, God help us!' or 'The ladies, God bless them!'" Sayers saw, as Jesus' women followers saw, that Jesus had no fragile male ego that would cause him to put down women so that he could feel superior. "There is no act, no sermon, no parable in the whole Gospel that borrows its pungency from female perversity; nobody could possibly guess from the words and deeds of Jesus that there was anything 'funny' about woman's nature."[8]

The social surge tells us that Christianity inherently oppresses women and relegates them to second-class citizenship. Do we notice something of a parallel to the issue of Christianity and race? The charge of discrimination—based on sex and ethnicity—may be laid at the feet of Christendom, but not at the feet of Christ himself. Luminaries like Frederick Douglass saw the true Jesus that his slave masters had tried to obscure with lies. Sayers saw the true Jesus that misogynists tried to hide from her with similar-sounding mistruths. She, like Douglass, saw the difference in the Christ of the oppressor and the Christ of the liberated.

Expressions of Christianity have had human flaws. But the Christ upon which the message is based is perfectly human and perfectly God, and so no such flaw can be found in him. Indeed, he has seen our flaws yet offers to clothe us in his perfection so that we might stand before God, every one of us, free, equal, and valued.

AN INVITATION TO IDENTITY

The morning of that women's conference in Lima, Peru, arrived. I had flown in the night before, thinking almost solely about the event. I was only to speak for about ten or fifteen minutes, yet it seemed like a herculean task. Looking back, I think that the brevity is what made it seem so impossible. Jesus had so much to say to and about women that it seemed impossible—unfair even—to expect me to convey the depth and beauty of what he said in just fifteen minutes.

Humility washed over me before I could step out onto that stage, however. I wasn't the sole voice at that conference. Others, including and especially women, would have far more time and opportunity to share the biblical message about the value of womanhood. Indeed, a particular woman who wasn't Peruvian—and who wasn't even at the conference—would end up communicating to them better than I ever could. That woman was my assistant, Tara.

Tara's spiritual journey through abuse and discovery had personally inspired me (and continues to inspire to this day). Before my trip, she provided me with a written account of how she had found her true identity amid the suffering, degradation, and pain of prolonged and systematic abuse. Exaltation of her status as someone valued and loved by the Source of all reality had now filled what was once a pain-wracked void. Knowing how afraid I felt and how inadequate for the task, she permitted me to share her thoughts with the Peruvian women that day. As I mentioned previously, when I tried to wrap my mind around this invitation, I found two voices. The first was Jesus' voice; the second was Tara's.

As I stepped onstage, with typical Peruvian passion, the audience overwhelmed me in a tidal wave of applause. I took the microphone and shared a few introductory pleasantries and comments before getting to the heart of what I was compelled to share—a woman's invitation to true and equal identity in Christ.

"Women between the ages of forty and fifty-five are the most invisible population of the Christian church," Tara had written. "This is largely dependent upon their lack of identity. The church tends to focus on young adults, as they are the future of the church. The elderly are the history of the church. The church also focuses greatly on men as the head of the household, and on married couples having a 'godly' marriage. If you were to ask women, though, about who they were, they would identify themselves as wives, mothers, workers." Whether coming from the secular world or the church, many a woman finds her identity not by who or what she is, but by her relationships with others, usually men or children.

Tara had overcome years of physical and emotional abuse. Given what I had learned about the experiences of many Peruvian women, I wondered how many in that audience had firsthand knowledge of the kind of experience I was recounting for them. She had survived the trauma and found herself living what seemed like a storybook life. "At thirty-eight years old, I loved my life. I had been married sixteen years to a husband I adored. I had three beautiful teenagers that were growing up faster than I could blink." How many in that audience wished for such a deliverance? Life seemed deep and enriching, at least on the surface. And then she disclosed the deeper reality. "Life was great," she wrote, "except I had no idea who I was."

The once roiling auditorium had become silent, a cathedral of attention. Every woman knew where the story could go. "That same year my husband left me for a younger woman. I was devastated beyond comprehension. I was left with a question I now could not answer. With my kids being almost grown, and my no longer being a wife, who was I?" Defining ourselves by our relationships to other people and by our duties will inevitably leave us hollow.

"It took an amazing and unforeseeable journey over the next four years to finally be able to answer that question," Tara continued. "I learned that who I am is not based on who I was married to. It is not based on who my children are or what type of house I have or job I do. Who I am is based on one thing and one thing alone. My Father. My identity rests in being the daughter of a King."[9]

For many of the women in that auditorium, when I read that last statement, an exuberant "Amen!" was quick in coming. Having a heavenly Father who loves us infinitely and unconditionally is readily welcome news, isn't it? I recall as a Muslim that I once thought it an unspeakable blasphemy for any human being to call God their "Father." Such a statement came dangerously close to equating our imperfect human natures with God's perfect nature. Yet as I studied what it means for a Christian to call God "Father," I began to see that there is no ontological equivalence being espoused. Rather, God acts toward us like a father, caring for our needs in an intimate way, seeking our well-being and disciplining us when necessary for our benefit. In Islam God is distant, aloof, wholly "other." While Islam registers human love for God and God's thorough knowledge of human beings, we are to remain in our places as Muslims—ones who submit to God's will. He is the Master, we are the slaves, and that's as far as the relationship goes. The gospel offers the enticing picture that God is more than just a will to be followed. He is a person to be adored and to have relationship with. Worshiping God as Father invites fulfillment, not just obedience. It invites us into an identity beyond that of a slave.

Before I went out on that stage, I prayed that I might say something of value to those women and that the letter I was going to read would give them hope. Yet I couldn't help but wonder if the letter's excitement about calling God "Father" might be off-putting for some women in that audience. For too many women, *father* is a leaden concept. Perhaps one woman didn't feel her father's affection unless she acted properly. Perhaps another's father physically or emotionally abused her, leaving her to feel objectified and worthless. Perhaps yet another saw her dad beat her mother. Perhaps hearing over the years that God is their heavenly Father became something like background noise that no longer evoked enthusiasm, if it ever did.

But Tara's letter, her delight in finding an unchanging identity in God her Father, spoke to the Peruvian women who—like so many of us—find their sense of identity shifting with the sands of circumstance. She added, "My identity rests in my Savior, Jesus Christ. The world is filled with roller coaster rides, ups and downs, joys and tragedies. It can change in a second." A truer statement is hard to find. "My Father's love for me is the one thing though that doesn't change. It is constant. He loves me more than anything I can imagine or comprehend. Nothing I do or don't do is a requirement for that. Nothing I do can ever make me deserving of it, but he gives it freely to me anyway." The unchanging status of divine love is based on the unchanging nature of the Divine Being. His perfect nature entails stable character. His stability leads to security.

And security in knowing our worth leads to security of identity, come what may.

My short time with those dear women culminated in a crescendo with the final words I read from Tara's letter. "It was only when I embraced this truth that I was able to experience peace for the first time in my life. True peace and comfort of knowing that through all my victories and my defeats I am truly enough." The tsunami of applause this letter and its message received dwarfed the tidal wave of welcome that came fifteen minutes earlier. This woman, who had been trafficked as a sex slave and literally treated like a commodity, had found that she belonged to no one save the one who gave his all for her sake. I had been wondering what I could offer an auditorium full of Peruvian women. I had nothing to offer them except two people who would matter more. A fellow woman, who has endured such devaluing pain that it is a wonder she has found the strength to survive, let alone thrive in her God-given identity. And Jesus, the one who secured that identity.

John Greenleaf Whittier saw the transcendent beauty of womanhood shouting out to the world through the gospel, far above the culture's demoralizing din. He gifted us these verses about the God-given gift of womanhood:

> Oh, dwarfed and wronged, and stained with ill,
> Behold! Thou art a woman still!
> And, by that sacred name and dear,
> I bid thy better self appear.
> Still, through thy foul disguise, I see
> The rudimental purity,
> That, spite of change and loss, makes good
> Thy birthright-claim of womanhood;

An inward loathing, deep, intense;
A shame that is half innocence.
Cast off the grave-clothes of thy sin!
Rise from the dust thou liest in,
As Mary rose at Jesus' word,
Redeemed and white before the Lord!
Reclaim thy lost soul! In His name,
Rise up, and break thy bonds of shame.
Art weak? He's strong. Art fearful? Hear
The world's O'ercomer: "Be of cheer!"
What lip shall judge when He approves?
Who dare to scorn the child He loves?[10]

This is the gift I want my daughters to embrace—a gift I am not qualified to bestow but I am charged to encourage. That gift is an identity rooted not in circumstances or performance, not in beauty or physical fitness. Indeed, their identities are not even rooted in their self-determination. Their liberty comes from being anchored in the Source who determined the existence of all things. That is a glorious hope, is it not? A woman's identity is not determined by her contributions to her family, society, or even her own well-being, as wonderful as those things may be. Such a truth frees her, as it does all of us, from self-loathing when she messes up. Her identity and value—just as much as mine—is moored to the one who is incapable of messing up.

The ballet that is Jesus' last few days of earthly ministry is quite a marvel to behold. Women stood by him and ministered to him even as he was being tortured and led down the path, carrying his cross toward the place where excruciating torture would end his life. Women were there for him at the cross. They would eventually realize that Jesus was on the cross for them.

Women rose early in the morning to anoint his buried body at the tomb. What they encountered was an empty tomb from which the Savior had already risen to anoint those women with honor and eternal life.

Jesus is not the founder of a man's religion. He is the foundation upon which all human value, for both men and women, is built. He invites men to find their identities in him and emulate his life of lifting women to their rightful places as men's equals. He invites women to root their identities in him. It is a bold invitation that takes courage to accept. When the world tells us—especially women—that we only find value and worth through achievement and status, Jesus liberates from that trap. Women don't have to achieve to discover themselves. They can achieve because they already have found themselves in God.

PART 3

NOT MERELY RELIGION

CHAPTER 8

THE PERSON IN WHOM WE FIND THE ANSWERS

BEYOND RELIGION

"What if I told you that Jesus came to abolish religion?" That is the opening line of Jefferson Bethke's 2012 spoken word YouTube video "Why I Hate Religion, but Love Jesus."[1] Both the title and the opening line have evoked quite a response, judging by the 34.9 million views it has received as of this writing. *Religion* has become something of a dirty word in Christian circles, which is ironic. The popular notion—with which I share some affinity—is that religion is a set of laws or rules that govern how humans interact with a particular deity and with each other, such that following the rules earns one a place in heaven or at least favor with the deity. Humanity, in its attempts at self-justification, has been busy creating rule-based religions.

It has been popular in Christian circles to claim that "Christianity isn't a religion; it's a relationship." I've even said something similar in sharing my story of how I went from the religion of Islam to a relationship with Christ. I put it that way often and purposefully instead of saying "from Islam to Christianity" to communicate that Christianity invites us into an intimate and immanent relationship with God that goes beyond the Creator-creation dynamic. The gospel—the good news—is that we no longer have to be burdened with perfect or near perfect obedience to laws, rules, or rites of atonement to have salvation.

Yet Bethke's video garnered criticism as well as praise. Christians pointed out that the New Testament specifically uses the word *religion* to describe something good, not hate-worthy. In the book of James, we read, "Religion that is pure and undefiled before God the Father is this: to visit orphans and widows in their affliction, and to keep oneself unstained from the world" (James 1:27). Pure religion isn't ritualism, it's faith put into action to serve God and others. And in the verse just prior, James counts religiosity as worthless if it isn't accompanied by a truthful heart and a restrained tongue (v. 26). Still other critics took issue with Bethke's rhetorical question, "What if I told you Jesus came to *abolish* religion?" by pointing out Jesus' words that he *did not* come to abolish the law, but to fulfill it (Matt. 5:17). Keep in mind that Bethke was trying to communicate in a four-minute video that there is an important distinction between a religion that teaches strict adherence to earn one's salvation and a gospel-centered relationship that ought not lead to self-righteousness. He clarified much of this in a forty-five-minute video of a sermon describing more thoroughly the difference between rules-based religion and grace-based relationship.[2]

While it is fashionable for Christians to believe that their faith is not based on religiosity, the broader culture begs to differ with them. Amid the increasingly vitriolic culture wars, battle lines have been drawn, usually quite distinctly by Christians, who seek a return to family values of the "good ol' days" while decrying the growing liberalism in the West. Outside the Christian fold, the culture depicts Christians as narrow-minded, judgmental people who long for the old days that weren't all that good for ethnic minorities and women. To be a Christian, so the broader culture thinks, one has to follow arbitrary rules, belong to a sheltered group, and judge others as less morally upright. This creates a sad obfuscation of the gospel message, which is that no one—regardless of ethnicity, creed, or gender—is righteous enough to spend eternity with God. Yet God has given his Son as the means to have Jesus' righteousness imputed to us even as our sin is imputed to him. Thus, if religious observance and pietism doesn't achieve salvation, it certainly doesn't entitle a person to judge others for being less observant or pietistic. And yet the broader culture deems Christians to be among the most self-righteous and thus judgmental of people.

There is yet another irony here. By categorizing Christians in these ways, the broader culture engages in the very judgmentalism it condemns. My friend, Vince Vitale, has pointed out that people are increasingly offended by almost everything while forgiving almost nothing. In an age where everything you say can and will be used against you in perpetuity, thanks to the internet, judgmentalism is practically a birthright. Both the church and the broader culture are guilty of the sins they charge each other with, calling to mind images of pots and kettles.

Sometimes, however, this assessment of Christians is spot-on correct. In fact, James addresses partiality and favoritism in the very chapter in which he discusses pure religion. "Show no partiality

as you hold the faith in our Lord Jesus Christ, the Lord of glory"
(James 2:1). He instructs believers not to favor the rich over the poor.
This suggests that classist thinking is antithetical to the Christian
gospel of God's unmerited, impartial grace. And if that's true, then
it's easy to see that racist and sexist thinking are incompatible with
the gospel message as well. Indeed, I hope we've seen just that in the
previous chapters. Rules-based, pietistic religion leads to justification of self, as well as the vilification of and separation from others.
By contrast, the gospel has no place for our self-justification and
thus cannot make room for divisions or vilifications.

The central truth around which all others orbit in the Christian
faith is that God in his holiness must necessarily judge our sin yet
in his compassion still provide a way to restore our once Edenic
relationship with him. This is what makes Christianity more than a
religion. I have argued numerous times that all religions are *not* the
same. While they have some similarities, they are essentially different. They differ on what God is like, if there are multiple gods, and
even if there are any gods. They fundamentally disagree on what
explains our origins and what explains the human condition. The
chasm of difference is indeed wide. And yet the world's various religions are bound by a common cord: they teach that human beings
have to prove themselves worthy of heaven, enlightenment, or whatever the ultimate prize may be. Consequently, self-righteousness and
self-exaltation inevitably swell. Christianity stands out in its reduc-
tion of the swelling because salvation does not come when we have
worked hard enough to please God, but when we trust the pure work
God has done to save us. Every human is equally in desperate need
of a savior—yet every human is so desperately loved that God has
provided that Savior, without favoritism. This truth entails that no
one—not one—is entitled to view anyone else as lesser or less worthy.

While this truth alone has not been enough to unite us in ending racism and sexism, it has served as a catalyst to break the walls of tribalistic religiosity that breed division. "Religion has been a source for change in American race relations, from abolition to the Civil Rights movement. Thus, religion can provide the moral force for people to determine that something about their world so excessively violates their moral standards that they must act to correct it," write Michael Emerson and Christian Smith.[3] But what has hindered American Christianity from doing so across ethnic lines (and by logical extension, gender lines) isn't the gospel message itself, but the religious structure through which it is either expressed or, in some cases, suppressed. "Far from knocking down racial barriers, religion generally serves to maintain these historical divides, and helps to develop new ones."[4] Why? Perhaps because humans have a natural bent toward rules-based religiosity that leads to group identity, which in turn causes us to value religious form over spiritual substance. "Our" kind of worship is the right kind, for example. Everyone else's is either too emotional or not emotional enough. Religiosity, coupled with a history we have a hard time owning up to, keeps Sunday segregated. This form of religion, not the pure religion that seeks the welfare of others and restrains our self-serving attitude, is the kind of religion Jesus did, in fact, come to abolish.

While I'm convinced that there's something about the gospel that distinguishes Christianity's message from Christendom's past, I'm more firmly convinced that the *someone* at the center of the gospel message distinguishes following Christ from surrounding oneself in the trappings of Christianity.

Bethke's video attracted responses from beyond his own Protestantism. A Muslim created a viral video just five days later and modeled it after Bethke's.[5] It's a poetic espousal of Islamic doctrine and a polemic against Jesus' deity, the Trinity, and the cross. While it doesn't actually address the same point Bethke was making, it's fascinating that both Bethke and this Muslim focused on Jesus, specifically his nature and character.

Jesus tends to pop up (and usually take center stage) whenever religious discussions happen, regardless of which religions are at issue. He's a prophet to Muslims, an incarnation of Vishnu to Hindus, a bodhisattva to Buddhists, and a sage to Taoists. Even the most ardent skeptic might refer to Jesus as an example of morality. Why the clamor to adopt Jesus as our own, regardless of our worldview? One can only speculate. But my suspicion is that it is hard to fight the gravity of his personage. We all perceive, even if in just a peripheral way, that Jesus transcends rules-based religion. The gospel message of which he is the center brings that peripheral perception into direct focus by augmenting religion with a relationship. Leaders of nearly every religion have brokered a relationship between their faith and Jesus. Perhaps the reason is that he seeps into the culture's ethnic and gender fissures more than we might realize.

Here's an anecdotal example. In pre-lockdown 2020, I spoke in an open forum at a major American university. An engaging woman originally from a Muslim country in Africa stood in the growing line during the Q&A period. When she came to the microphone, she was witty and winsome, stealing the audience's heart. She had been exploring the Christian faith in comparison to the religion of her birth and hashed out the differences with her family. Understandably, given her religious background, even though she found Jesus as described in the Bible to be compelling, her watershed issue was the deity of Christ. She asked, "Can I love Jesus and still serve Allah?" What a fascinating way to frame the issue. Religiously, she wanted to know if Christianity and Islam were at loggerheads. Existentially, she couched the "religion versus religion" question in terms of her love of Jesus—as a person.

I had to explore this aspect further by asking her a question of my own. "When you say you love Jesus, what do you mean?" I asked this because many Muslims claim to love Jesus (as happened in the Muslim response to Bethke's video), but what they mean is that they admire him as a prophet. Her answer was even more remarkable than her initial question, revealing much about her past, one in which brides could readily be joined with four other women in marriage to one man. "I just love that he says, 'Husbands love your wife like I love the church.'"

It weighed on her that in the dominant religion of her home-land, men can have up to four wives while women can have only one husband. This had been her experience since she was born. And yet something in Jesus' character as described in the Bible drew her in. He spoke and acted in ways that affirmed her equality with men. He proved that she had inestimable worth on a divine scale.

When she said that she loved the way Jesus commanded husbands to love their wives just as Christ loves the church, she partially quoted what the Bible says. Even that partial truth offered enough light to direct her to the source of luminance. The full verse, I pointed out to her, commanded that husbands love their wives as Christ loves the church "and gave himself up for her" (Eph. 5:25). This self-sacrificial orientation of Jesus—of the God of the Bible—sets him apart. Indeed, it does more.

As she well knew, Muslims believe that God, *Allah*, is the greatest possible being. This is why they frequently say in prayer and in common speech *Allahu Akbar*, which means "God is Greater." Since

God is the greatest possible being, it stands to reason that he would express the greatest possible ethic. That ethic, the Somali woman readily agreed, is love. Love was the center of the verse that enamored her with Jesus in the first place. But one more implication remains. As the greatest possible being, God would express love as the greatest possible ethic in the greatest possible way. This follows because the greatest possible being wouldn't be a being of moral half measures, but of the greatest possible measures. And what is the greatest possible way to express love? It is obviously self-sacrifice. That which reasoning and theology demand, Calvary's cross supplies.

Jesus' sacrificial love is what the Somali woman had been looking for, and it extended far beyond the self-sacrifice of a husband for his (one) wife. Yes, such a man should never think of his wife as somehow lesser. Indeed, if he is to give up his life for hers, he must value her more. This mirrors Jesus' heart for each of us.

Why does this excursus matter in a book about ethnicity, gender, and faith? Because Christianity, if it is to be more than a white man's religion, must be more than another religion. It must be based on an intimate and immanent relationship with the Divine. The transcendent being, who indiscriminately gives of himself to the world, serves as the model for which men ought to think of and treat women and for which people of every ethnicity must treat all others. When we hem in that truth with religious strictures that divide, we miss the glory of what might be.

JUST SHINE

A video I saw of two women makes me strongly suspect that something like this religious hemming happened to them. They recorded a one-hour video of their respective journeys away from "born-again Christianity" to lives devoid of religious faith. But their conversation was not typical of others I've seen between atheists who left the Christian faith. Usually these video testimonies will criticize Christianity for a lack of evidence or logic. While they mentioned this briefly, the women took a different approach, focusing instead on their experiences of "deconversion."

There were many waves on the sea of their wide-ranging critique of Christianity, but the undercurrent of critique was that Christianity imposes a social bubble by which Christians end up being friends only with other Christians, shielding themselves from people who think or act differently. They also described a legalistic religiosity that dominated even their sincerely felt relationships with Jesus. These may have been their experiences, but not the experiences of multiplied millions of Christians living around the world, many as minorities in hostile areas. But we can learn from these women's experiences, which might be particularly prominent in Western countries. Christianity's transformation into tribal Christendom creates a bubble that seals us off from others. The danger is that division—ideological, social, religious, and ethnic—can easily be established before we even realize it. And yet Christianity, when understood and lived as Christ commissioned us, doesn't insulate itself from the world. "Go therefore and make disciples of all nations," Jesus commissioned (Matt. 28:19). It's hard to do that and not encounter those who don't look or think differently.

There is another lesson we can learn from these two women's experiences of Christianity-turned-tribal-Christendom. The chief criticism they had against "born-again Christianity" was that it was characterized by dos and don'ts and a core doctrine that almost robbed them of their identities as authentic humans. The interviewer explained, "So many people would say, 'Christianity is wonderful and it's beautiful.' To that I would say, 'You don't know what Christianity is. The core beliefs of Christianity teach you things that make you feel disgust in others and in yourself for being a natural human being.'" Her guest readily agreed. Indeed, the doctrine of sin is what had begun to unravel her guest's faith. She found herself suddenly crying as she was teaching children about sin, looking at a little girl and unable to tell that little girl that God found her to be morally filthy. This, in their words, was the false narrative of Christianity that they were now liberated from. Christianity is a "strict set of beliefs that revolve around the ideology that you are a sinner, that you need to be saved," the host said. "And without the grace of God, you are worthy of suffering. That's it. That's what born-again Christianity is. That's pain."[6] That's quite the indictment.

The problem, of course, is that the false narrative they both rejected is only half the narrative. I can only speculate, but they seem to have been taught only (or at least mostly) that humans are sinful without the simultaneous truth that men and women are equally made in God's image. I must assume that they truly had religious experiences dominated by judgment and self-loathing.

That deprivation is a tragedy indeed. And I fear that the deprivation they experienced is all too common. We say things like "We are made in God's image" so commonly that we skim past the requisite awe that the concept should kindle in our hearts and minds. Analogies in life might help but don't really come close. Imagine if, as a young basketball player, Michael Jordan were to come up to you as you played a pickup game and told you that you remind him of himself when he was your age. The intoxicating encouragement would linger for weeks if not longer. Imagine that you're an artist and a well-known art critic admires your work as reminiscent of Renoir's. Would you not bask in the comment? If you sing and a talent scout says that you have the chops of an Adele, would your confidence not skyrocket? These accolades and compliments are nothing compared to being called the divine image bearer. Why? Because the source of all existence, the very well from which all things flow, tells you and me that we bear God's image. Theologians have analyzed what that means for centuries, and as valuable as their understandings have been, the reality is that we don't need that level of depth before we should start to be awed by the very concept of being made in God's image. The source of all morality, intelligence, and goodness created us, regardless of color or sex, to reflect something of God's image. I had no hand in the creation of all things, yet as a created being, God has bestowed upon me the infinite value of reflecting the image of the Creator of all things. The wonderment of such a lofty concept led King David to declare that God made humanity "a little lower than the heavenly beings and crowned him with glory and honor" (Ps. 8:5). Carolyn Custis James points out that this translation actually falls a little short of the original intent. This verse could just as easily read that God made humanity "a little lower than God."[7]

As atheists, the women in the deconversion video rejected the idea of human sinfulness but ended up throwing out the fantastic and fantastically true counterpart, which is that we reflect the divine. Legalistic religiosity teaches us to see only sin in ourselves. In our effort to rise above that rules-based shame, we aggrandize ourselves through rule-following, only to see the sin in others as greater than the sin in ourselves. The gospel of grace teaches that sinfulness is not what was intended for us, that though sin may veil the *imago Dei*, the image persists. The veil that hides it has been torn asunder by the one who placed that image on us in the first place. That glorious, jaw-dropping truth somehow had been made mundane and boring, even irrelevant, to those two women. They now believe that since throwing off the idea that they are sinful, they can "just shine," to use their words. Yet it's impossible to shine brighter than the image of God we bear, bestowed on us by the Light of the World.

At the end of the video, both women were elated to have thrown off the shackles of their former faith, one declaring that "Life is good now," followed by the other exclaiming, "Life is so good after Christianity!" Their elation seems to contradict Peter's answer to Jesus when asked if he would abandon Jesus. "Lord, to whom shall we go?" Peter asked. "You have the words of eternal life" (John 6:68). The distinction between what those two erudite women said and what Peter said deserves notice. The women seem to experience a good life *after Christianity*. Peter's answer, however, didn't suggest that there was any place to go outside of Christendom as a mere religion. He said that Jesus himself, not a religiosity loosely based on his words—held the key to real life. Legalistic Christianity may result in the kind of straitjacket the women had escaped. But the person of Jesus offers truth that sets us free to be what we were intended to be.

The alternative is a life that may be good for some but terrible for others, with no real hope of something better. Some years ago, the British Humanist Association tried to popularize the idea that life without God can be liberating and enjoyable. They plastered the sides of double-decker buses with billboards that read, "There's probably no God. Now stop worrying and enjoy your life." But Julian Baggini, the thought-provoking atheist thinker, exposed the superficiality of that notion. "Atheists should point out that life without God can be meaningful, moral and happy. But that's 'can' not 'is' or even 'should usually be.' And that means it can just as easily be meaningless, nihilistic and miserable." He continues, "Atheists have to live with the knowledge that there is no salvation, no redemption, no second chances. Lives can go terribly wrong in ways that can never be put right. Can you really tell the parents who lost their child to a suicide after years of depression that they should stop worrying and enjoy life?"[8]

Among the many things that caught my attention in this video was the fact that the women had been so entrenched in a rules-and-restrictions religion that they couldn't see that they may have exchanged one form of bondage for another, secular one. If one's self-worth depends on how well one shines, then our metrics become performance, possessions, and prestige. We still seek self-justification, but now it is measured by human standards, subject to change as culture changes. It's still tribal and legalistic. The world demands that we be successful, educated, helpful, politically correct, and in love. Otherwise, what are we? The freedom to shine becomes the obligation to shine. That burden doesn't sound the least bit light.

That is the very opposite of the freedom the gospel gives us. In Christ we don't perform good works to get saved. We perform good works in reaction to being saved. We don't shine to get God's attention and favor. We shine in the light we already have from God's attention and favor. In Christ, not ourselves, we find the Light of the World who shines through us by his own merit. "The people who walked in darkness have seen a great light," the Bible tells us (Isa. 9:2; Matt. 4:16). Jesus' perfection allowed him to bear our burdens on the cross, freeing us from the obligation to pay our infinite debt to God incurred by our sin. He bids us to throw off the worldly yoke of shining to the level acceptable by the media, our peers, and even ourselves and take upon our shoulders his yoke. "For my yoke is easy, and my burden is light," he tells us (Matt. 11:30). That's more than religion.

At one point in the video, the interviewer recounted the trauma of leaving her former faith and let out, "Oh my God," but then quickly caught herself. "I mean, I should say, 'Oh my dog,'" she quipped. Obviously, she wasn't calling out to a deity she doesn't believe in; she was just repeating a colloquialism. But it brought to mind a poem I recently read about doubt in God's existence, and how the uncertainty actually is a clue to God's existence. It is titled "Staying Power."

"STAYING POWER"

In Appreciation of Maxim Gorky at the
International Convention of Atheists, 1929

Like Gorky, I sometimes follow my doubts
outside and question the metal sky,
longing to have the fight settled, thinking
I can't go on like this, and finally I say
all right, it is improbable, all right, there
is no God. And then as if I'm focusing
a magnifying glass on dry leaves, God blazes up.
It's the attention, maybe, to what isn't
there that makes the notion flare like
a forest fire until I have to spend the afternoon
spraying it with the hose to put it out. Even
on an ordinary day when a friend calls,

tells me they've found melanoma,
complains that the hospital is cold, I whisper, God.
God, I say as my heart turns inside out.
Pick up any language by the scruff of its neck,
wipe its face, set it down on the lawn,
and I bet it will toddle right into the godfire
again, which—though they say it doesn't
exist—can send you straight to the burn unit.
Oh, we have only so many words to think with.
Say God's not fire, say anything, say God's
a phone, maybe. You know you didn't order a phone,
but there it is. It rings. You don't know who it could be.
You don't want to talk, so you pull out
the plug. It rings. You smash it with a hammer
till it bleeds springs and coils and clobbered up
metal bits. It rings again. You pick it up
and a voice you love whispers hello.[9]

God has a way of sticking in our psyches even when our religion disappears. When we reject him, somehow he still beckons. Even in the act of doubting his existence, we may end up calling to him. This doesn't prove that he exists, of course. But it points to the human longing to connect with the transcendent. C. S. Lewis and others have argued that for every legitimate need or desire, there always seems to be a fulfillment. Our seemingly incidental calls to God, even a God we don't believe in, signals a legitimate need. Religion that breeds self-righteousness, judgment, self-loathing, and separation doesn't satisfy that need; it only amplifies it.

The person of Christ encompasses the place that inspires the pure religion that James encourages but transcends it to create relationship with each one of us. Connection with God is a legitimate need. Christ is the legitimate fulfillment. I went from rules-based religiosity to grace-based relationship. When my mind lingers on the deconversions the women shared in that video, I'm struck by the juxtapositions of our journeys. As a Christian whose faith centers on a relationship beyond religion, I reject the same religiosity they rejected. The relationship with Christ they somehow missed is the relationship I, a former religionist, embraced.

The Somali woman who engaged in dialogue with me at the open forum saw that Christianity offers something beyond religion. It offers a person—a fully divine yet fully human person. Jesus is olive-skinned, yet his life has changed the Western world. God has no ethnicity, and while his incarnation in Jesus had a Jewish ethnicity, as the first of a new humanity he belongs to all ethnicities. Jesus was a man, yet women found in him the honor and dignity their sexist cultures denied them or made elusive.

THE CENTRAL FIGURE

Historically, movements for social change have centered around a charismatic figure, sometimes more than one. When such figures—like Nelson Mandela, Mahatma Gandhi, or Susan B. Anthony—arrive on the scene, they evoke visceral reactions in others. In some bellies, the fires of hatred ignite at the very mention of their names. In others, the fires of inspiration warm their hearts at the sound of their speeches. While these personalities polarized and catalyzed many people, the causes for which they stood and even died did not depend on them.

Consider then, that Jesus was and has been admired by so many (but not all) such activist figures. What does it tell us that they, with their cause-inspiring prowess, found inspiration from Jesus, an itinerant preacher from a forsaken Roman province? Could it signal that the nature of his personhood—not just the force of his personality—is the fount of inspiration for all causes of justice and equality? Could it be that the gospel—a message centered around this person—goes beyond mere religion? And could it be that a message whose center is a person—not an ideology or method—is the message we need as the foundation from which to seek and secure justice and equity for all persons?

A TONIC OF BIG THINGS

F. W. Boreham's essay "A Tonic of Big Things" discusses how therapeutic it can be to have our seemingly small, separate lives lost in exploration of the big things of existence. He tells the story of Professor Henry Drummond and four companions sailing on the coast of West Africa. The men could barely speak one another's language. One pulled out a Bible and happened to open it to John 3:16, the famous verse that reads, "For God so loved the world, that he gave his only Son, that whoever believes in him should not perish but have eternal life." Another man raced to get his own Bible, then another, until they all retrieved their Bibles. As they read together, a common language formed because the immensity of what Scripture says to all of us about objective equal human value translates well. "Men can see the mountain-peak over a multitude of intervening obstacles," Boreham observed. "And no obstacles of race or language, rank or station, can preclude men from the fellowship of life's immensities. 'They shall cry unto the Lord, and

He shall send them a Saviour, and a great one!' Everything in the gospel is 'a tonic of big things.'"[10]

There remain big things to address and big obstacles to surmount when it comes to ethnic and gender equality. The tonic that helps us address these big things is the biggest message ever delivered to the world: the gospel of equality. In today's globalized world, we have to scale language barriers of all kinds, but the figurative ones are the highest. The word *justice* has lost any sense of commonality. Conservatives suspect that the word is a mask for Marxism or socialism. Liberals suspect that conservatives don't mean justice for all, but justice for some. Even the word *gospel* has been politicized and weaponized so that anyone bearing the label *evangelical* is stigmatized as a fundamentalist or Christian Nationalist. "Progressive Christian" doesn't refer to a Christian interested in social progress, but to a person who employs an anemic theology to push a social agenda that has higher priority than the gospel message. "Conservative Christian" means someone who sacrifices social issues on the altar of theological fealty. We can scale the barrier when we see that rich theology can vault us to social progress. We do not see each other clearly because we do not listen to each other at all. The obstacles of language and agenda do, in fact, preclude us from the fellowship of life's immensities. What I have proposed here is what Boreham proposed long before me: that the common ground and the true grounding of the gospel can help surmount the intervening obstacles. Is that a contradiction, given that not even Christians seem to agree with each other? Perhaps in practice, but not in principle.

Tribal Christendom is a maze of division. But Christianity as an allegiance to the person whose nature, character, and work changed the world is a flower bed. Beautiful flower beds are mosaics of diversity. Different flowers bloom at different times, in different shades, and at different heights. Yet all draw from the same soil, the same water, and the same sun. There is unity amid the diversity. The quests for racial and gender equity present us with big things. But the objective morality that drives the imperative for us to fix these big things is based in the tonic of the gospel message. God is the necessary being from whom all existence—material, spiritual, and moral—flows. The gospel message is that the God who needs nothing to explain his existence loves all of us equally with an ineffable intensity. This is where mere religion tends to fall short. Religions describe either a single deity too lofty to directly connect with humanity's ills or tell tales of multiple gods whose characters are worse than our own.

Religion that builds bridges is active religion, modeled after the character and actions of the one upon whom the religion is founded. In the New Testament, James interestingly preludes his description of valuable and true religion by coupling action and belief: "Be doers of the word, and not hearers only, deceiving yourselves. For if anyone is a hearer of the word and not a doer, he is like a man who looks intently at his natural face in a mirror. For he looks at himself and goes away and at once forgets what he was like. But the one who looks into the perfect law, the law of liberty, and perseveres, being no hearer who forgets but a doer who acts, he will be blessed in his doing" (James 1:22–25).

But what are we to hear and then do? In a world where we should have found ourselves enlightened by now to have outgrown racism and sexism, we still dwell in their darkness. We are to shine the light, in word and deed, that reflects the powerful vulnerability Christ lived out in elevating women and challenging ethnic prejudice. Religious rules won't inspire that. But he can.

Let us resist the cultural surge to get on the train that relegates

Christ to a historical figure who may have said and done some good things once. Let us resist the even stronger urge to get on the train that would lead us to decry Christianity as a white man's religion that inspires racism and promotes sexism. The doors have opened to us to get on the train that leads us to look to the olive-skinned, black-haired, transcendent person of Jesus, who offers us more than a white man's religion.

ACKNOWLEDGMENTS

My wife, Nicole, was an encouragement and a source of insight and strength as I wrote this book. Her support during the most challenging eighteen months of our lives is testimony to the fact that she is a true spiritual warrior without whom I would not have accomplished much, let alone written a book. She has my unending gratitude. In that similar vein, my children have endured and seen much. They, too, have been pillars of support and sources of inspiration on top of just being great kids with whom to experience life. If there is anything of value you read in these pages, you have my wife and children to thank for much of it. And I have God to thank for them.

This book owes much of its content to my dear friends Derek Caldwell, who helped me tremendously with research and editing, and Brandon Cleaver, whose thoughtful sharing of insights and experiences as an African American Christian have shaped my thinking for the better. Derek and Brandon were so very generous in giving me their time. I pray that the words between these covers honor their contributions.

I'm also grateful to Randy Pistor for providing research help from time to time. Cameron McAllister and I also shared occasional conversations about race and faith during some of the most turbulent times in the summer of 2020. Our conversations blessed me enormously and made their way into my times in front of the keyboard.

I'm grateful to Zondervan, particularly Stan Gundry and my editor Ryan Pazdur. Both of them were patient, gracious, and understanding when challenges arose during the course of writing. Ryan's contributions both over the phone and in his edits to the manuscript have enriched this book greatly.

Of course, many others with whom I've conversed (usually over a meal) have shaped my thinking, but I fear I might miss some names if I start to list them. Christopher Brooks, a true statesman for the gospel and equality, has so blessed my life that even our casual conversations have been influential. Lisa Fields's courageous graciousness has been invaluable as well.

For two previous books, my assistant, Tara Ehrhardt, assisted me in entering edits and changes, sometimes for hours at a time. But with this book, due to various restrictions and life circumstances, she was not able to express her inexplicable gift of translating my indecipherable handwritten edits into typewritten text. Yet her contributions to this book have been far more profound. Her story, although mentioned briefly, has not only made its way into these pages but has also influenced the thoughts expressed in the chapters on women. My former colleagues from RZIM and I have carried much pain in recent months. But Tara has had to relive some of her past trauma. I would not have wanted that for her for any reason. Yet she has told me that she has seen God work through her pain for his good purposes. Indeed, I have seen her minister to others in their pain more effectively than ever. One way in which God has used her pain is to shape what you hold in your hands, dear reader.

NOTES

Preface

1. Diane Langberg, *Redeeming Power: Understanding Authority and Abuse in the Church* (Grand Rapids: Brazos, 2020), xi.
2. Diane Langberg makes this observation about how Jesus transformed the heart of Zacchaeus in *Redeeming Power*, 174.

Chapter 1: Seeing the Social Surge

1. Tom Holland, *Dominion: How the Christian Revolution Remade the World* (New York: Basic Books, 2019).
2. I'm half Polish, but I was raised within an Arab-American culture.
3. Ibram X. Kendi, *How to Be an Antiracist* (New York: One World, 2019).
4. Martin Luther King Jr., *Letter from a Birmingham Jail*, quoted in *Letters to a Birmingham Jail: A Response to the Words and Dreams of Dr. Martin Luther King, Jr.*, ed. Bryan Loritts (Chicago: Moody, 2014), 20.
5. Anthony B. Bradley, ed., *Aliens in the Promised Land: Why Minority Leadership Is Overlooked in White Christian Churches and Institutions* (Phillipsburg, NJ: P&R, 2013), 15.
6. See Holland, *Dominion*.
7. Dennis Prager, "Can We Be Good without God?," Pragertopia, March 3, 1993, https://pragertopia.com/unlimited-program/the-oxford-debate-can-we-be-good-without-god/.
8. Douglas Murray, *The Madness of Crowds—Gender, Race, and Identity* (London: Bloomsbury, 2019), 291.

Chapter 2: Defining the Objection

1. Throughout Scripture, we see that those of ethnicities outside of the Hebrews played crucial roles, including well before Jesus' earthly ministry. As but one example among many, in Jeremiah 38:4–13, we read the account of an Ethiopian named Ebed-melech who rescued the prophet Jeremiah from dying alone in an empty cistern after being thrown in there by the king's henchmen.

2. See Elizabeth Isichei, *A History of Christianity in Africa: From Antiquity to the Present* (Grand Rapids: Eerdmans, 1995), 31.

3. Michael J. Kruger, "The Church in Her House: The Dynamic Ministry of Women in Early Christianity," The Gospel Coalition, June 14, 2018, https://www.thegospelcoalition.org/conference_media/church-house-dynamic-ministry-women-early-christianity.

4. Rodney Stark, *The Triumph of Christianity: How the Jesus Movement Became the World's Largest Religion* (New York: HarperOne, 2011), 65.

5. Stark, 186.

6. Stark, 198.

7. Philip Jenkins, *The Lost History of Christianity: The Thousand-Year Golden Age of the Church—and How It Died* (San Francisco: HarperOne, 2008), 3, quoted in Stark, *Triumph of Christianity*, 212.

8. To be accurate, the Roman Empire was an equal-opportunity conqueror in that it didn't target darker skinned countries but sought to conquer and assimilate everyone.

9. David Bentley Hart, *Atheist Delusions: The Christian Revolution and Its Fashionable Enemies* (New Haven, CT: Yale University Press, 2009), 167–68.

10. Hart, 32–33.

11. Hart, 32–33.

12. "Tom Holland Tells NT Wright: Why I Changed My Mind about Christianity," Unbelievable?, YouTube, July 17, 2018, https://www.youtube.com/watch?v=AIJ9gK47Ogw.

13. Tom Holland, *Dominion: How the Christian Revolution Remade the World* (New York: Basic Books, 2019), 25.

14. Will Durant, *Caesar and Christ: The Story of Civilization*, vol. 3 (1944; repr., New York: MJF Books, 1993), 652.

15. Soong-Chan Rah, *The Next Evangelicalism: Freeing the Church from Western Cultural Captivity* (Downers Grove, IL: InterVarsity, 2009), 16.

16. Rodney Stark, *The Triumph of Faith: Why the World Is More Religious Than Ever* (Wilmington, DE: ISI Books, 2015), 16.

17. Stark, 18.

18. Stark, 21–22.

19. Lamin Sanneh, *Whose Religion Is Christianity? The Gospel beyond the West* (Grand Rapids: Eerdmans, 2003), 41.

20. Sanneh, 36.

21. Stark, *Triumph of Faith*, 139.

22. Stark, 74–76.

23. Stark, 84.

24. Kruger, "Church in Her House."

25. "Satellite TV, Social Media Fuel 'World's Fastest Growing Church' in Iran," Religion News Service, October 20, 2020, https://religion news.com/2020/10/20/satellite-tv-social-media-fuel-worlds-fastest -growing-church-in-iran/.

26. Caleb Parke, "Iran Has World's 'Fastest-Growing Church,' Despite No Buildings—and It's Mostly Led by Women: Documentary," Fox News, September 27, 2019, https://www.foxnews.com/faith -values/worlds-fastest-growing-church-women-documentary-film.

27. Michael O. Emerson and Christian Smith, *Divided by Faith: Evangelical Religion and the Problem of Race in America* (New York: Oxford University Press, 2000), 3.

28. Jemar Tisby, *The Color of Compromise: The Truth about the American Church's Complicity in Racism* (Grand Rapids: Zondervan, 2019), 86–87.

29. I'm indebted to Dr. Esau McCaulley for his insights on how the

divide formed between conservative and liberal theologians' views on the Bible and social activism.

30. Leonard Ravenhill, *Why Revival Tarries* (Grand Rapids: Bethany House, 1959), 48.

31. Tisby, *Color of Compromise*, 19.

Chapter 3: The Moral Heart of the Social Matter

1. See Sam Harris, *The Moral Landscape: How Science Can Determine Human Values* (New York: Free Press, 2010).

2. Sam Harris, *Free Will* (New York: Free Press, 2012).

3. Charles Darwin, *The Descent of Man, and Selection in Relation to Sex*, vol. 1 (New York: D. Appleton and Company, 1871), 193.

4. Richard Weikart, *From Darwin to Hitler: Evolutionary Ethics, Eugenics, and Racism in Germany* (New York: Palgrave Macmillan, 2004), 232–33.

5. Michael Ruse, "God Is Dead. Long Live Morality," *Guardian*, March 15, 2010, https://www.theguardian.com/commentisfree /belief/2010/mar/15/morality-evolution-philosophy.

6. "Martin Luther King Jr.—Acceptance Speech," The Nobel Prize, December 10, 1964, https://www.nobelprize.org/prizes/peace/1964 /king/26142-martin-luther-king-jr-acceptance-speech-1964/.

7. Hitler's quote is found on a plaque at the memorial at Auschwitz. Scott Boeser, "The Slovakia Experience: A Journey in the Land of Castles," *Scott Boeser* (blog), October 2, 2008, http://scottboeser .blogspot.com/2008_10_01_archive.html.

8. "Martin Luther King Jr.—Acceptance Speech."

9. Martin Luther King Jr., *Letter from a Birmingham Jail*, quoted in *Letters to a Birmingham Jail: A Response to the Words and Dreams of Dr. Martin Luther King, Jr.*, ed. Bryan Loritts (Chicago: Moody, 2014), 23.

10. Carl Ellis Jr., *Free at Last? The Gospel in the African American Experience* (Downers Grove, IL: InterVarsity, 1996), 23.

11. For an engaging analysis of the miracle motif and white evangelical belief in it as a way to end racism, see Michael O. Emerson and

Christian Smith, *Divided by Faith: Evangelical Religion and the Problem of Race in America* (New York: Oxford University Press, 2000), esp. chap. 6.

12. Jörg Nagler, "Abraham Lincoln's Attitudes on Slavery and Race," *American Studies Journal* 53 (2009), www.asjournal.org/53-2009 /abraham-lincolns-attitudes-on-slavery-and-race/.

13. Nagler.

14. The debate took place on July 13, 2017. The following recollections of the exchange are from my own notes taken at the debate.

15. Ruse, "God Is Dead."

16. Ibram X. Kendi, *How to Be an Antiracist* (New York: One World, 2019), 13.

17. Kendi, 20, emphasis added.

18. Kendi, 23.

19. Kendi, 206.

20. Kendi, 208.

21. Kendi, 23.

22. John Perkins, "Why We Can't Wait for Economic Justice," in *Letters to a Birmingham Jail: A Response to the Words and Dreams of Dr. Martin Luther King, Jr.*, ed. Bryan Loritts (Chicago: Moody, 2014), 45.

23. Perkins, 46.

24. See Robin DiAngelo, *White Fragility: Why It's So Hard for White People to Talk about Racism* (Boston: Beacon, 2018).

25. DiAngelo, 142.

26. DiAngelo, 68.

27. The full account of Tom's transformation is chronicled in Thomas A. Tarrants, *Consumed by Hate, Redeemed by Love: How a Violent Klansman Became a Champion of Racial Reconciliation* (Nashville: Thomas Nelson, 2019).

28. C. S Lewis, "Christian Apologetics," in *The Timeless Writings of C. S. Lewis: God in the Dock* (New York: Inspirational Press, 2003), 363.

29. John Greenleaf Whittier, "The Cross," in *Whittier's Complete Poetical Works* (Boston: Houghton, Mifflin, 1895), 192.

Chapter 4: Scripture, Slavery, and Race

1. Howard Thurman, *Jesus and the Disinherited* (New York: Abingdon-Cokesbury Press, 1949; repr., Boston: Beacon Press, 1996), 30–31.

2. Stuart George Hall, ed., *Gregory of Nyssa: Homilies on Ecclesiastes. An English Version with Supporting Studies*, Proceedings of the Seventh International Colloquium on Gregory of Nyssa, trans. Stuart George Hall (Berlin and New York: Walter de Gruyter, 1993), 73–74.

3. Steven Spielberg, dir., *Amistad* (Glendale CA: Dreamworks Pictures, 1997).

4. Robertson McQuilkin and Paul Copan, *An Introduction to Biblical Ethics: Walking in the Way of Wisdom*, 3rd ed. (Downers Grove, IL: IVP Academic, 2014), 453.

5. Paul Copan, *Is God a Moral Monster? Making Sense of the Old Testament God* (Grand Rapids: Baker, 2011), 125.

6. See Exodus 23:9 (you are not to oppress strangers); Leviticus 19:33–34 (treat strangers among you as equals); Leviticus 24:22 (equal treatment for all, Hebrew or foreigner); Numbers 15:15–16 (the law applies equally to Hebrew and foreigner, which might imply equal treatment, although there is a noted difference in the rules for foreign slaves); Deuteronomy 15:12–15 (specifically the verse that grounds their gentle treatment of slaves in Israel's own Egyptian bondage); and Deuteronomy 23:15–16 (specifically on treatment of slaves).

7. Copan, *Is God a Moral Monster?*, 454.

8. Copan, 136.

9. See Copan, 131, for examples.

10. W. E. B. Du Bois, *Black Reconstruction in America, 1860–1880* (New York: Free Press, 1998), 30.

11. Here I am not making a case for or against reparations. Rather, my intent is only to show that had we heeded biblical principles more closely at the time of Reconstruction and emancipation, we may not be engaging in reparations debates today. The Bible is blamed for creating problems that it actually solves.

12. Quoted in Esau McCaulley, *Reading While Black: African American*

Biblical Interpretation as an Exercise in Hope (Downers Grove, IL: IVP Academic, 2020), 146, citing Jacob Milgrom, "Leviticus 23–27," *Anchor Bible* 3b (New York: Doubleday, 2001), 2214.

13. *The Holy Bible: English Standard Version* (Wheaton, IL: Crossway Bibles, 2016).

14. McCaulley, *Reading While Black*, 159.

15. McCaulley, 161.

16. McQuilkin and Copan, *Introduction to Biblical Ethics*, 457.

17. Kristin Romey, "Living Descendants of Biblical Canaanites Identified via DNA," *National Geographic*, July 27, 2017, https://www .nationalgeographic.com/news/2017/07/canaanite-bible-ancient-dna -lebanon-genetics-archaeology/.

18. David M. Goldenberg, *The Curse of Ham: Race and Slavery in Early Judaism, Christianity, and Islam* (Princeton, NJ: Princeton University Press, 2003), 156.

19. If Genesis 9 is so clear, when and why did it get so derailed? As already mentioned, Goldenberg found that association of Ham with blackness began between the second and fourth centuries. Religious historian Stephen Haynes points out that early church fathers and rabbis alike started to link blackness with Ham's sin and punishment. Later medieval Christian and Jewish interpretations did the same. They may have done so, however, in light of an influx of darker-skinned slaves so that their linkage had more to do with attempting to make sense of the reality they saw before them rather than finding a justification for race-based subjugation. Stephen R. Haynes, *Noah's Curse: The Biblical Justification of American Slavery* (Oxford: Oxford University Press, 2002), 7.

20. Haynes, 7–8.

21. David Brion Davis, *Inhuman Bondage: The Rise and Fall of Slavery in the New World* (Oxford: Oxford University Press, 2006), 66–67.

22. McQuilkin and Copan, *Introduction to Biblical Ethics*, 455.

23. McQuilkin and Copan, 455.

24. McQuilkin and Copan, 456 (emphasis in original).

25. Laws of Hammurabi §§ 16, 170–71, 282.

26. Laws of Hammurabi §16, Laws of Lipit-Ishtar §12, Laws of Eshnunna §49–50, Hittite Laws §24, cited in Copan, *Is God a Moral Monster?*, 131.

27. For a more detailed discussion of these codes and a comparison with the Bible, see Copan, *Is God a Moral Monster?*, 87–100.

28. For detailed treatments of these issues, see Copan, *Is God a Moral Monster?*, chaps. 15–17; Paul Copan and Matthew Flannagan, *Did God Really Command Genocide? Coming to Terms with the Justice of God* (Grand Rapids: Baker, 2014). For a different perspective, see various articles by Clay Jones, including his "Killing the Canaanites: A Response to the New Atheism's 'Divine Genocide' Claims," January 31, 2011, www.equip.org/article/killing-the-canaanites/.

29. See John H. Walton and J. Harvey Walton, *The Lost World of the Israelite Conquest: Covenant, Retribution, and the Fate of the Canaanites* (Downers Grove, IL: IVP Academic, 2017), 169–90.

30. Ronald Behm and Columbus Salley, *What Color Is Your God? Black Consciousness and the Christian Faith* (Downers Grove, IL: InterVarsity, 1981), 20.

31. See Jemar Tisby, *The Color of Compromise: The Truth about the American Church's Complicity in Racism* (Grand Rapids: Zondervan, 2019), 70–87.

32. Frederick Douglass, quoted in Gene Andrew Jarrett, ed., *The Wiley Blackwell Anthology of African American Literature: Volume 1: 1746–1920* (Oxford: Wiley & Sons, 2014), 205.

Chapter 5: Jesus and Authentic Ethnic Equality

1. C. H. Spurgeon, "The Lamentations of Jesus," in *The Metropolitan Tabernacle Pulpit Sermons*, vol. 26 (London: Passmore & Alabaster, 1880), 661–62.

2. Spurgeon, 661–62 (italics added).

3. Several authors have written about how vital a role Christianity has played in bringing about such reforms, yet churches remain divided and haven't helped things socially progress. See Michael O. Emerson and Christian Smith, *Divided by Faith: Evangelical*

Religion and the Problem of Race in America (New York: Oxford University Press, 2000).

4. William Lane Craig, "Excursus on Creation of Life and Biological Diversity (Part 14): Etiological Motifs in Genesis 2," *Reasonable Faith*, June 2, 2019, https://www.reasonablefaith.org/podcasts /defenders-podcast-series-3/excursus-on-creation-of-life-and -biological-diversity/excursus-on-creation-of-life-and-biological -diversity-part-14/.

5. F. W. Boreham, "Our Rubbish-Heaps," in *The Luggage of Life* (New York: Abingdon, 1918), 147–53.

6. This prophecy came to pass in AD 70 when the Romans destroyed Jerusalem, including the temple.

7. Peter Farrelly, dir., *Green Book* (Hollywood, CA: Universal Pictures, 2018).

8. The social theory that has garnered more attention than others is critical race theory (CRT). For works by its proponents, see Richard Delgado and Jean Stefancic, *Critical Race Theory: An Introduction*, 3rd ed. (New York: NYU Press, 2017); Kimberlé Crenshaw, "Mapping the Margins: Intersectionality, Identity Politics, and Violence against Women of Color," *Stanford Law Review* 43, no. 6 (1991); Derrick A. Bell, *Race, Racism, and American Law* (Boston: Little, Brown, 1984). For a recent criticism of CRT, see Helen Pluckrose and James A. Lindsay, *Cynical Theories: How Activist Scholarship Made Everything about Race, Gender, and Identity—and Why This Harms Everybody* (Durham, NC: Pitchstone, 2020).

9. Crenshaw, "Mapping the Margins," 1297.

10. Blaise Pascal, *Pascal's Pensées* (New York: Dutton, 1958), 103.

11. See Getrude Himmelfarb, *The Roads to Modernity: The British, French, and American Enlightenments* (New York: Vintage, 2005), 116–30; Irv Brendlinger, "John Wesley and Slavery: Myth and Reality," Faculty Publications—College of Christian Studies, Paper 116, George Fox University, 2006, http://digitalcommons .georgefox.edu/ccs/116.

12. Steven Pinker, *Enlightenment Now: The Case for Reason, Science, Humanism, and Progress* (New York: Viking, 2018), 8.

13. Pinker, 11.

14. Jens Zimmermann, *Incarnational Humanism: A Philosophy of Culture for the Church in the World* (Downers Grove, IL: IVP Academic, 2012), 29.

15. Pinker, *Enlightenment Now*, 11.

16. Quoted in Craig Keener, "A Reassessment of Hume's Case against Miracles in Light of Testimony from the Majority World Today," *Perspectives in Religious Studies* 38, no. 3 (2011): 294.

17. John Gray, "Delusions of Peace," September 21, 2011, Prospect, www.prospectmagazine.co.uk/magazine/john-gray-steven-pinker-violence-review

18. Steven Pinker, *The Better Angels of Our Nature—Why Violence Has Declined* (New York: Penguin, 2011).

19. Marcello Pera, "How Necessary Is Christianity to European Identity?," Marcello Pera, January 26, 2011, http://marcellopera.it/index.php/it/sala-stampa/interventi/840-how-necessary-is-christianity-to-european-identity.

20. John Greenleaf Whittier, "Hymn," in *Whittier's Complete Poetical Works* (Boston: Houghton, Mifflin, 1895), 268–69.

Chapter 6: Challenging the Interpretations of the Texts That Challenge Us

1. James B. Hurley, *Man and Woman in Biblical Perspective* (Eugene, OR: Wipf and Stock, 2002), 16.

2. Hurley, 16.

3. Richard Dawkins, *The God Delusion* (New York: Mariner, 2008), 51.

4. For a deeper explanation of the Trinity, see chapter 9 of my book *Grand Central Question: Answering the Critical Concerns of the Major Worldviews* (Downers Grove, IL: InterVarsity, 2014).

5. Victor P. Hamilton, "Genesis," *Evangelical Commentary on the Bible*, vol. 3, ed. Walter Elwell (Grand Rapids: Baker, 1995), 13.

6. William Lane Craig, "Excursus on Creation of Life and Biological

Diversity (Part 14): Etiological Motifs in Genesis 2," *Reasonable Faith*, June 2, 2019, https://www.reasonablefaith.org/podcasts /defenders-podcast-series-3/excursus-on-creation-of-life-and- biological-diversity/excursus-on-creation-of-life-and-biological -diversity-part-14/.

7. Diane Langberg, *Redeeming Power: Understanding Authority and Abuse in the Church* (Grand Rapids: Brazos, 2020), 5.

8. Hurley, *Man and Woman in Biblical Perspective*, 23.

9. Hurley, 23.

10. Hurley, 27.

11. Richard M. Davidson, *Flame of Yahweh: Sexuality in the Old Testament* (Grand Rapids: Baker Academic, 2007), 303, 342–43.

12. Davidson, 219–21.

13. Hurley, *Man and Woman in Biblical Perspective*, 37–39.

14. Hurley, 39–40.

15. Hurley, 40.

16. Davidson, *Flame of Yahweh*, 511.

17. Davidson, 511, quoting Jacob Milgrom, *Leviticus 17–22: A New Translation with Introduction and Commentary*, Anchor Bible 3A (New York: Doubleday, 2000), 1807. Davidson notes, however, that there could be a social stigma attached if the raped woman was the daughter of a priest.

18. Davidson, 535.

19. Paul Copan, *Is God a Moral Monster? Making Sense of the Old Testament God* (Grand Rapids: Baker, 2011), 119–20.

20. See Davidson, *Flame of Yahweh*, 359, 519.

21. Davidson, 242.

22. Three in particular that I would like to recommend are the three quoted in this section: Hurley's *Man and Woman in Biblical Perspective*, Davidson's *Flame of Yahweh: Sexuality in the Old Testament*, and Copan's *Is God a Moral Monster? Making Sense of the Old Testament God*.

23. Hurley, *Man and Woman in Biblical Perspective*, 75.

24. Hurley, 75.

25. "Tom Holland Tells NT Wright: Why I Changed My Mind about Christianity," Unbelievable?, YouTube, July 17, 2018, https://www.youtube.com/watch?v=AIJ9gK47Ogw.
26. Quoted in Hurley, *Man and Woman in Biblical Perspective*, 59–60.
27. Hurley, 62.
28. Quoted in Hurley, 62.
29. Quoted in Hurley, 62.
30. Quoted in Hurley, 63.
31. Quoted in Hurley, 72.
32. Philo of Alexandria, *The Works of Philo: Complete and Unabridged*, trans. Charles Duke Yonge (Peabody, MA: Hendrickson, 1995), 165.
33. Flavius Josephus, *Against Apion* 25.201, quoted in Hurley, *Man and Woman in Biblical Perspective*, 61–62. Josephus attributed this statement to the Old Testament, though it is nowhere to be found in the available manuscripts. Some debate whether Josephus actually wrote this passage.
34. Kathy Keller, *Jesus, Justice, and Gender Roles: A Case for Gender Roles in Ministry* (Grand Rapids: Zondervan, 2012), 9.
35. For a concise summary on the spectrum of views on gender roles in the church, see Michael F. Bird, *Bourgeois Babes, Bossy Wives, and Bobby Haircuts: A Case for Gender Equality in Ministry* (Grand Rapids: Zondervan, 2012), 11–14. This is part of a series called Fresh Perspectives on Women in Ministry, which includes Keller, *Jesus, Justice, and Gender Roles*, and John Dickson, *Hearing Her Voice: A Case for Women Giving Sermons* (Grand Rapids: Zondervan, 2012).
36. Bird, *Bourgeois Babes*, 28.
37. Renate Viveen Hood, "Women in the Bible" in *The Lexham Bible Dictionary*, ed. John D. Barry et al. (Bellingham, WA: Lexham, 2016), citing Rose Sallberg Kam, *Their Stories, Our Stories: Women of the Bible* (New York: Continuum, 1995).
38. Bird, *Bourgeois Babes*, 30–31.
39. Hurley, *Man and Woman in Biblical Perspective*, 214.
40. Hurley, 214–15.
41. Philip B. Payne, *Man and Woman, One in Christ: An Exegetical*

and Theological Study of Paul's Letters (Grand Rapids: Zondervan, 2009), 405–15.

42. See Bird, *Bourgeois Babes*, 27.
43. This ethic of male service tempers other biblical references in which Paul called on women to be in submission to their husbands, as in Colossians 3:18–19 and Titus 2:5.
44. Hurley, *Man and Woman in Biblical Perspective*, 148.
45. This is a far cry from directing a woman to stay in an abusive situation. Peter calls for submission to win the man who doesn't obey the Scriptures, not a man given to mental or physical abuse. Such sin is abhorred by God (Ps. 11:5). Further, Peter's remark in verse 7 that the wife is the "weaker" partner should be viewed within this four-corners context. She isn't weak in a spiritual sense, or else her godly example would fail to persuade her disobedient husband to submit to Christ. Instead, "weaker" may refer to comparative physical weakness or comparative societal weakness given the challenges women faced at that time. What we can say definitively is that "weaker" does not refer to women being ontologically lesser.
46. Keller, *Jesus, Justice, and Gender Roles*, 10.
47. See Bird, *Bourgeois Babes*, 25, 39–43.
48. Keller, *Jesus, Justice, and Gender Roles*, 13.
49. Hurley, *Man and Woman in Biblical Perspective*, 199.
50. Philip H. Towner, *The Letters to Timothy and Titus*, New International Commentary on the New Testament (Grand Rapids: Eerdmans, 2006), 220. The question of how women are to be "saved through childbearing" in 1 Timothy 2:15 has been one of great curiosity through the centuries. Philip Payne believes that Paul highlighted childbearing as an allusion to the fact that Jesus was born of a woman, assuring his readers that women belong to an equal class of people that can be saved (Payne, *Man and Woman, One in Christ*, 440–41). Paul was speaking to women who may have sought outside assurance of their value, perhaps by returning to their former paganism. Linda Belleville is helpful here, as she points out that women in this culture may have been turning back

to the Ephesian cult of Artemis, a Greek goddess who allegedly ushered women safely through the childbearing process (Linda Belleville, "Women in Ministry: An Egalitarian Perspective," in *Two Views on Women in Ministry*, ed. Stanley N. Gundry and James R. Beck [Grand Rapids: Zondervan, 2005], 99).

51. Towner, 15.

52. Ben Witherington III, *Women and the Genesis of Early Christianity* (Cambridge: Cambridge University Press, 1992), 196.

53. Witherington, 196. See also Bird, *Bourgeois Babes*, 41.

54. Payne, *Man and Woman, One in Christ*, 395–97.

55. Linda Belleville, "Teaching and Usurping Authority: 1 Timothy 2:11–15," in *Discovering Biblical Equality: Complementarity without Hierarchy*, ed. Ronald W. Pierce and Rebecca Merrill Groothuis (Downers Grove, IL: InterVarsity, 2004), 205–23.

Chapter 7: When God Puts Women in Their Place

1. Malcolm Gladwell, "The Hug Heard Round the World," *Revisionist History* (podcast), Pushkin, accessed November 3, 2021, https://www.pushkin.fm/episode/the-hug-heard-round-the-world/.

2. Rosabeth Moss Kanter, "Some Effects of Proportions on Group Life: Skewed Sex Ratios and Responses to Token Women," *American Journal of Sociology* 82, no. 5 (1977): 965–90, http://www.jstor.org/stable/2777808.

3. Her comment is found in an interview with Kathleen Nielson about Severance's book. The interview is found at Kathleen Nielson, "Women in the Tapestry of Christian History," The Gospel Coalition, June 24, 2012, https://www.thegospelcoalition.org/article/women-in-the-tapestry-of-christian-history/. Severance's book is *Feminine Threads: Women in the Tapestry of Christian History* (Fearn, Ross-shire, Scotland: Christian Focus, 2011).

4. Gary A. Rendsburg, "Unlikely Heroes: Women as Israel," *Bible Review* 19, no. 1 (February 2003): 16, https://jewishstudies.rutgers.edu/docman/rendsburg/184-bible-review-unlikely-heroes-women-as-israel/file.

5. Richard Bauckham, *Gospel Women: Studies of the Named Women in the Gospels* (Grand Rapids: Eerdmans, 2002), 12.

6. Andrew E. Hill and John H. Walton, *A Survey of the Old Testament*, 3rd ed. (Grand Rapids: Zondervan, 2009), 251.

7. Ephrem the Syrian, quoted by George R. Beasley-Murray, *John*, Word Biblical Commentary 36 (Waco, TX: Word, 1987), 66.

8. Dorothy L. Sayers, *Are Women Human? Penetrating, Sensible, and Witty Essays on the Role of Women in Society* (Grand Rapids: Eerdmans, 2005), 68–69.

9. For the permission to quote these comments here and to share them in Peru, I am deeply grateful to Mrs. Tara Ehrhardt, a true survivor.

10. John Greenleaf Whittier, "A Woman," in *Whittier's Complete Poetical Works* (Boston: Houghton, Mifflin, 1895), 450.

Chapter 8: The Person in Whom We Find the Answers

1. Jefferson Bethke, "Why I Hate Religion, but Love Jesus," YouTube, January 10, 2012, www.youtube.com/watch?v=1IAhDGYlpqY&ab _channel=Jeff%26Alyssa.

2. Jefferson Bethke's clarification video can be viewed here: "My Heart behind 'Why I Hate Religion, but Love Jesus,'" YouTube, March 11, 2012, https://www.youtube.com/watch?v=dN1iyJQGrcU.

3. Michael O. Emerson and Christian Smith, *Divided by Faith: Evangelical Religion and the Problem of Race in America* (New York: Oxford University Press, 2000), 18.

4. Emerson and Smith, 18.

5. Talk Islam, "Why I Hate Religion, but Love Jesus, Muslim Version, Spoken Word, Response," YouTube, January 15, 2012, https://www .youtube.com/watch?v=YNGqrzkFp_4.

6. Questioning the Narrative, "Christian Deconversion Testimony, Former Born-Again Christian," YouTube, October 21, 2018, https://www.youtube.com/watch?v=Ku2foeCIBys.

7. Carolyn Custis James, *Half the Church: Recapturing God's Global Vision for Women* (Grand Rapids: Zondervan, 2010), 54–55.

8. Julian Baggini, "Yes, Life without God Can Be Bleak. Atheism

Is about Facing Up to That," *Guardian*, March 9, 2012, www
.guardian.co.uk/commentisfree/2012/mar/09/life-without-god
-bleak-atheism.

9. Jeanne Murray Walker, "Staying Power," in *New Tracks, Night
Falling* (Grand Rapids: Eerdmans, 2009), 54–55. Used with
permission.

10. F. W. Boreham, *The Luggage of Life* (New York: Abingdon, 1918),
184.

Saving Truth

Finding Meaning and Clarity in a Post-Truth World

Abdu Murray

*Untangle from a culture of confusion and find
hope in the clarity that Christ offers*

Western culture embraces confusion as a virtue and decries clarity as a sin, especially with regard to sexuality, morality, identity, and religion. *Saving Truth* by Abdu Murray describes how we arrived at this stage and provides winsome arguments and touching stories to offer clarity to a culture that rejects but desperately needs truth.